Refugee on the Threshold

A True Story

Timothy Leacock

ISBN 979-8-89112-166-9 (Paperback)
ISBN 979-8-89112-168-3 (Hardcover)
ISBN 979-8-89112-167-6 (Digital)

Copyright © 2024 Timothy Leacock
All rights reserved
First Edition

All rights reserved. No part of this publication may be reproduced, distributed, or transmitted in any form or by any means, including photocopying, recording, or other electronic or mechanical methods without the prior written permission of the publisher. For permission requests, solicit the publisher via the address below.

Covenant Books
11661 Hwy 707
Murrells Inlet, SC 29576
www.covenantbooks.com

For people fleeing persecution and those who care for them

and

For Meseret, Zahra, Abdulrahman, and Sherifa

Uncertainty and fear and ignorance
about immigrants,
about people who are different,
has a history as old as our nation.

—Luis Gutierrez

Contents

Author's Note ix
Acknowledgments xi
Abbreviations xiii
Prologue xv

Chapter 1:   He Knows What to Do 1
Chapter 2:   Escape 10
Chapter 3:   Two Rivers 16
Chapter 4:   Land of the Free 21
Chapter 5:   Meadows County Corrections 29
Chapter 6:   Befriended...36
Chapter 7:   Well-Founded Fear 47
Chapter 8:   On the Threshold...56
Chapter 9:   Don't You Have Some Place Else to Live? 71
Chapter 10: Justice Will Prevail 76
Chapter 11: Day after Day 83
Chapter 12: Bare Necessities 86
Chapter 13: Why Are You Here? 92
Chapter 14: One Foot in the Doorway 98
Chapter 15: Intimidation..108
Chapter 16: Nexus 121
Chapter 17: The Last Straw 131
Chapter 18: Liberty 139
Chapter 19: Our Home Is Your Home......................................143
Chapter 20: Mom and Dad 152
Chapter 21: Intensive Supervision...162
Chapter 22: Pursuit of Happiness 164
Chapter 23: When Two Elephants Fight 170

Chapter 24: You Will Know What to Do 177
Chapter 25: Days of Uncertainty 183
Chapter 26: He's Not Here Right Now 187
Chapter 27: Home of the Brave 189
Chapter 28: Front Door or Back Door 194
Chapter 29: Export and Import 197
Chapter 30: Relationship 203

Epilogue 207
Postscript 211
Appendix A: Al-Shabaab 213
Appendix B: Types of Asylum 215
Appendix C: Regarding Ahmed 219
Reference List 223

Author's Note

This is the true story of a man seeking asylum, told through his eyes and those of a few witnesses to his struggle. All the events are true.

I used transcribed voice recordings to write this story. The content of letters and emails has been slightly edited for clarity.

All people's names and certain identifying details have been changed in order to disguise their identities and protect their privacy. Any resulting resemblance to actual persons is unintentional. "Meadows County, Iowa," and "Arabella, Iowa," are imaginary but represent actual places in the American Midwest.

Acknowledgments

This book would not be in its current form without the contributions of my beta readers, who gave me comments, critiques, questions, and insights that helped me make revisions to better present this story. I owe a debt of gratitude to the following writers, authors, and editors for reviewing my manuscript: Effie Caldarola, Lisa Kelly, Thomas Kelly, Donna Leacock, Matt Leacock, John O'Keefe, and Alice Sudlow. I wish to also thank Carl Malischke for his careful reading and providing insights into the immigration court system.

I am extremely grateful to David Rose, an excellent freelance editor, whose expertise and kind assistance helped bring my manuscript to the next level.

And finally, I value the contributions of Ruth Scherer Leacock, my wife, whose support and encouragement kept me writing. And I am most grateful to her for her recollection of details concerning many of the events in this story.

Abbreviations

AIDVP	Arabella Immigrant Detainee Visitor Program
AJFI	Arabella Justice for Immigrants
BBC	British Broadcasting Corporation
BIA	Board of Immigration Appeals
CAT	Convention against Torture
CBP	Canadian Border Patrol (Canada)
CBP	Customs and Border Protection (USA)
DHS	Department of Homeland Security
DNI	Director of National Intelligence
DOJ	Department of Justice
DRC	Democratic Republic of the Congo
EAD	Employment Authorization Document
EOIR	Executive Office for Immigration Review
ERO	Enforcement and Removal Operations
FBI	Federal Bureau of Investigation
GED	General Educational Development
HIAS	Hebrew Immigrant Aid Society
ICE	Immigration and Customs Enforcement
IDP	internally displaced person
INA	Immigration and Nationality Act
INS	Immigration and Naturalization Service
ISAP	Intensive Supervision Appearance Program
MCC	Meadows County Corrections
NCTC	National Counterterrorism Center
UNHCR	United Nations High Commissioner for Refugees
USCIS	US Citizenship and Immigration Services

Prologue

One action can dictate your whole future.

—Hadinet Tekie

Annie

2005—Kampala, Uganda

Paul and Estelle were asleep with their three young boys in their little house in Kampala, Uganda. It was midnight, a night darker than most. No kerosene lanterns alight, no streetlights, no moon. Barred windows had heavy drapes to keep out the mosquitoes. The single door was ill fitted and had some gaps on one side. Through one of these, a rubber hose was protruding.

Someone with a petrol can and a funnel was outside the door. The petrol made a faint drip-splash sound in the sitting room. Paul woke up, took a moment to recognize the sound, and started shouting, banging on the door. Soon, he had aroused the entire neighborhood from its slumber.

In the almost total darkness, the would-be assassin had set the petrol container on the ground and quietly slipped away.

Before daybreak, my friend Estelle called me. "Annie! They tried to burn us!"

"Who? What are you talking about?" I was immediately awake.

"They found us, someone searching for Paul, someone from Congo. The militia wants his life now in revenge for his escape."

"We'll help you, your whole family," I assured her. *But how could we help?*

Estelle sounded frantic. "We don't know what to do! Now that they found us, it's certain they will be back."

"You can live with us!"

That seemed to calm her. I was not thinking about what might happen should the dangerous men find them with *us*. But I knew in my heart that this was the time for action, to help them in any way I could.

That same morning, my husband (Michael) and I got to work with a plan to move Paul and Estelle's family to our apartment across the city. With the help of a Jesuit friend, Fr. John, we hired a truck and loaded it with the family's furniture and other possessions. They settled into our rented house with its extra bedroom. They had no income. They shared our home and ate with us as part of the family.

Like others on our hill, a brick-and-mortar wall enclosed our house. The wall had jagged glass sticking up at the top to discourage any thieves who might prowl at night. Because of the bars on the windows, it felt claustrophobic, like we were in prison. Our neighbors had night guards with rifles, often catching up on their sleep on shift. Plenty of guard dogs were in the neighborhood, dozing lightly. They were not pets. The glass-topped wall and watchful dogs protected us well.

*****

Paul and Estelle were lawyers from the Democratic Republic of Congo (DRC), their native country. Their work included defending the land rights of clients and reporting on human rights abuses to international organizations. One day, a militia group abducted Paul. They forced him to work in one of the mines, extracting rare minerals for markets in the West. Estelle went to the local authorities to fight for his release. But they would not listen; they just ignored her.

Estelle was loudly vocal. She had embarrassed the government officials who were afraid to confront the militia forces that had abducted Paul. After many days, Estelle's friends convinced her to flee. Because she was demanding action, her life was now in danger. She escaped to neighboring Uganda with her two young boys. She was pregnant with a third.

After working the mines with other enslaved men for a year, Paul got sick, and a militiaman took him to a hospital. He escaped from his captors and found Estelle and his boys in Kampala. They named the newborn Jean, after Fr. John, the Jesuit who had helped them.

*****

After many days of hiding at our house, Paul appeared to grow restless, agitated about his family's future. He made a few trips on his own to a representative of the United Nations High Commissioner for Refugees (UNHCR) and a lawyer with the Hebrew Immigrant Aid Society (HIAS). On one of these trips, Paul stepped into a *matatu*, a minibus taxi, usually overcrowded with over a dozen passengers. But he was not careful, did not pay attention. When he boarded at a busy stop, only three men and the driver were aboard. As they started moving, Paul suddenly realized the trouble he was in. They were speaking French and from the DRC, in league with the militia looking for him. The matatu traveled many kilometers and finally stopped in a secluded area. The militiamen forced him out. Paul suspected they would take him off the road, into the bush, and silently kill him.

"Empty your pockets," one of them said in French.

Paul took out his phone and handed it over. Then while they were distracted, he reached into his pocket again and triggered a piercing alarm. The men looked confused. They panicked and ran.

The alarm unit was simple. Michael had purchased it for his own use before coming to Africa, at a home-improvement store in Arabella, Iowa. It was the kind you put on windows: two magnetic pieces that, when separated, would activate. Hell, it was loud!

*****

A few days later, I received a call from Paul's stolen phone. The assassins must have been going through the numbers on his contact list, including mine. "Is Paul there?" a man asked.

"I don't know any 'Paul,'" I said and quickly hung up. I set down the phone, crossed my arms, and started pacing around the sitting room. Then I went to find Michael.

When I came back a short while later, our Uganda colleague's friend Haley had picked up my phone and called the number back. I heard her say, "I know a Paul." She did not have a clue of the danger she was placing Paul in.

I confronted Haley. "Do you know what you did?"

Haley's eyes got big. "Well, there's another Paul on the hill."

Mortified, our colleague Joseph said, "There's. No. Other. Paul!"

We had to pack up the family again to move them elsewhere. Joseph, Michael, and I found a place. We resettled the family in a town that was a suitable distance from Kampala.

*****

Michael and I had been living in Uganda, leading an NGO (nongovernment organization) that provided computer labs, maintenance training, and Internet connectivity to secondary schools in Uganda, Kenya, and Tanzania. After two years, Joseph took over East Africa operations, and we found ourselves out of a job there with no more productive reasons to stay. We prepared to leave for the States but would be back again each year to help Joseph receive shipments, touch base with him, and visit the many friends we made.

During our time in Uganda, Estelle became my friend. We had spent many months working together on behalf of her church group of thirty Congolese refugees. I was providing articles and stories on spirituality that she translated into French.

Not long after we headed back home that year, Estelle, Paul, and their three boys immigrated to a French province of Canada as refugees. I had played a role in keeping them safe, but HIAS made their dreams come true: a land of freedom to start anew, a safe place for their kids, and no more worries of abduction or worse. The family has settled, both parents have jobs, boys are in school, and they now have a baby sister born in Canada.

*****

How far would you go to save someone in danger? I have had to ask myself that question twice in my life.

Estelle was my friend. Thus, her family was special to me. When they were in immediate peril, I could act to help them, to save them. I was in unambiguous circumstances, faced with a life-and-death situation. Without taking much thought to the risks and the consequences for myself, I acted in their behalf. Not only that, I involved my husband in my plan.

There were no assurances of success, no obvious outcome. Yet I felt compelled to act for Estelle's family as if they were my own. This challenging experience was significant then, but I did not know how my reaction would change me and prepare me for what happened ten years later back home.

1

He Knows What to Do

> Man alone chimes the hour. And because of this,
> man alone suffers a paralyzing fear that no other
> creature endures. A fear of time running out.
>
> —Mitch Albom, *The Time Keeper*

Ahmed

I am part of the *diaspora*, those who left Somalia during the civil war in 1993. When I was only eighteen years old, I went to Ethiopia, where I met Zoya, my future wife. It was love at first sight. We were married three months later, and I became like a son to her father. My father died in the war when I was sixteen, and my mother died when I was a little kid, only eight then.

But my family never accepted Zoya even though she converted to Islam one month after we were married. Religion wasn't an issue for us; we were so in love. But because she was Ethiopian, the men in my family gave me two choices: divorce her or be expelled from the family. My family was extremely conservative. It was a horrible decision to make for one so young, but I chose Zoya and have never regretted it. She has been, for me, a gift from God.

We planned to leave Ethiopia four years later when the war started there. War was all around us; there was no end in sight. I went to South Africa, where they were accepting refugees without putting them in camps. It took twenty-three days to travel by car. I wanted to spare Zoya the long journey, so I went alone to check the place out and get an apartment and a job. Zoya flew there to join me the following year.

The UNHCR was paying South Africa to accept refugees, but there was no chance for citizenship. We had to register as refugees every six months. The country and the people did not want us there, but they gladly accepted payment from the UN and did not tell us where to live, and there was no war and no famine. It was the best we could do.

We settled in a district of Johannesburg, where apartments were cheaper, where some other Somali refugees lived, and close to the Indian quarter where poor people from India had settled. We raised our three kids there. They went to school, and Zoya took care of the household. I worked at many different jobs, and I managed to go to school part-time.

Where we stayed was called "the Locations." It was in Pretoria, South Africa, an area set aside for black African refugees, an unfriendly place to live. The people of Pretoria never accepted us—refugees with no status, no rights. We were outsiders. They treated us with suspicion and even hatred because we were taking away jobs, such as they were. There was xenophobia between blacks from different ethnic groups, and there was violence and constant crime, where robbers would take your money in the daytime with others watching and no help from the police.

I ran a shop for a time where I sold food and household items. Robbers attacked me and stole my money eight times. Once, they shot me in the leg. When one time I stood up to the robbers, they came back at night and burned my shop.

The violence, the robbing, and the unsafe conditions kept my whole family stressed out. Zoya could not sleep, and her blood pressure went up. Something had to be done. *Should we go back to Somalia?* My home country still had its problems, but I knew that my sister Fawzia and her husband would welcome us even after all this time. We had been living in South Africa now for nineteen years.

*****

March 27, 2016—Jowhar, Somalia

Leaving Zoya and the kids behind for now, according to our plan, I took a flight from Johannesburg and arrived in Mogadishu, Somalia. My brother-in-law Omar met me at the airport, and together, we traveled to my hometown of Jowhar. It was a big homecoming. I had not seen Fawzia for an extremely long time.

She embraced me with much joy. I felt like a little kid again. Fawzia was my big sister, my closest family, older than me by ten years, who had taken care of me after our mother died.

I was welcome to stay with them for as long as it took to get settled. I had phoned her every week or so over the years I was gone, but being together in one place was special. We talked about everything and shared a delicious meal.

Omar knew of an administrative, clerical position at the largest hospital in Jowhar. The hospital was government run. Getting that job was my dream. I thought that once I got the job, I could move Zoya and the kids back to Somalia so we could at least live together peacefully, and I could benefit from my job qualifications. My family depended, for now, on a friend, a former employer, a benefactor who helped them survive.

*****

I woke up full of hope and anticipation. The sky was clear, and a gentle wind was kind as I walked to the city center with my application papers in my hand. I observed the trees growing beside the river, the deep green color of their leaves. It was like I saw their beauty for the first time. Nothing felt real. My heart was so light.

My thoughts turned to Zoya. I wished she were here. I would show her my home, where I grew up, and all the places that were dear to me.

The renovated hospital looked very different. It was freshly painted and had a tiled entryway and large double doors at the entrance. When I arrived at about ten o'clock, other applicants were in line, three just inside the small waiting room and three more outside. I greeted them. While waiting, I noticed seven names on the bulletin board on the outside wall, my name among them. The notice read, "On the 28th of March, there will be seven candidates who will come to be interviewed." I was not too concerned about the competition since I was well qualified and could read, write, and speak English besides Somali, my native tongue.

Out of the corner of my eye, I saw a dark-red car quietly coast to a stop very close to our group. The driver wore a mask. Two men got out of the back. Both had their faces covered and wore black trousers and black shirts. They approached the four of us who were standing on the dirt road outside. Neither masked man said anything, but their eyes were intense as they studied us. Our group was silent as well. I stared back, not knowing what to expect.

The masked men were empty-handed, but I suspected they had weapons in the car. My heart started racing, and I wanted to run, but their glare kept me motionless and helpless. The younger one stepped up and dropped four envelopes on the ground in front of us, one at each man's feet. Satisfied with their mission and not saying a word, they returned to the car and slowly drove off.

We all stood there and looked at each other, silently trying to gauge each other's thoughts. My hands started shaking as I opened my letter. I read the single page and looked up at the other men to see grim looks on everyone. We compared our letters. They were identical: "You have 24–36 hours to leave Somalia or face the consequences." There was a black flag symbol stamped in the upper left corner I recognized as a mark of Al-Shabaab. How they wrote the letters, the Somali words they used at the beginning and the end and the signature, left us no doubt that these letters were from Al-Shabaab.

I quickly realized the reason they singled us out was because we were interviewing for a job with the government at a government-run hospital, and Al-Shabaab hates and kills anyone who supports or is connected to the government. A feeling of dread washed over me. I could see that the others were terrified, like me. None of us could hide our fear and disappointment. We all had hoped that when we came back home to Jowhar, our hard work would truly benefit our families and contribute to our country. Now we were at the mercy of people without respect for human life.

One guy was crying. Another guy would talk and then was quiet for a few minutes, and he kept asking us, "Could you repeat what you said?" I could see that so many things were happening in his mind in that brief space of time. I was the same; I did the same. If someone were to cut one hair on my head, I would feel it. That's how present I was.

"In a life-and-death situation," I told them, "thinking about being killed is not going to help us in any way. How we can get out of this situation is far more important than what has happened."

Because of the nature of the incident, I could not disclose my next step. I did not know who was who, so it was a wait-and-see situation. Everyone was a closed book. I could blame no one for that, including myself.

The death-threat letter from Al-Shabaab was shocking; it was unreal. I froze, as if my mind was trying to think beyond my ability. So many thoughts and feelings were swirling. One question that rose to the surface was, *When would they return to start shooting?*

So I did not wait there for long, not over five minutes. I wished the others well. We all scattered in different directions. That was the last time I saw those guys. I needed to reach a safe place, my sister's house. I had nowhere else to go.

As I hurried, my kids, especially my youngest, entered my thoughts. I wanted to make them proud of their father. The last thing I wanted was for my family to find out that I had lost my life in Somalia, trying to provide them with a better future.

I did not regret the decision to come to Somalia because of what had happened in South Africa. I was shot in the leg, robbed eight times, and so many other bad things happened, so I didn't have much choice. I wished I had wings so I could have flown back to South Africa and be with my wife and kids. That was what my heart desired. To be with them was all that I truly wanted.

I walked as fast as I could without drawing attention, constantly checking over my shoulders, suspecting anyone who might walk toward me. The world felt so narrow. It squeezed me from all sides. I didn't know what to do.

When I arrived at Fawzia's house, she could see from my face that something terrible had happened. I was not smiling like I usually did when I greeted her. I came inside, still out of breath. "They want to kill me! Al-Shabaab found me waiting at the hospital, and they want to kill me!"

"What?" Fawzia gasped. "What are you talking about?"

"They gave me this letter. It says they will kill me if I don't leave the country."

"Show me the letter." She studied it and frowned. "You are correct. Oh, this is terrible. I will call my husband. He is at work now. We will figure something out."

Fawzia and Omar called an urgent family meeting that afternoon. My auntie joined the three of us at about three o'clock. We discussed the entire issue and incident.

"What did they look like? How were they dressed? What color were their clothes?" Fawzia asked.

"There were three. One guy was short and another tall, and one was driving the red car," I said. "They were dressed in black, had their faces covered, and wore sandals."

"What language were they using? Was there an accent? Was it the local dialect, and what did you understand?"

"They didn't say anything. They just dropped these letters at our feet."

As I answered other questions, I felt frustrated. Everything was happening very fast.

Fawzia's voice was agitated. She was stunned and full of sorrow at the same time. She recalled so many incidents: "Remember what happened to so-and-so, what happened to that lady, what happened to that man, how so-and-so had disappeared, how so-and-so had been killed in public, how so-and-so had been taken out from the house during the dark of night?" Fawzia and her husband supposed that all those incidents were somehow tangled together.

Fawzia continued, "And I don't have to tell you that two of my sister's husbands had been killed by Al-Shabaab. And I won't *ever* forget that they assaulted me in public and beat me up just for listening to the BBC, which was banned by Al-Shabaab." She was crying by this time.

The more we talked, the more senseless it all seemed. I was getting more and more frightened. I did not know that Somalia had gotten so terrible. So many innocent lives had been taken.

Finally, Omar told me, "This is not over. Surely, they will either find you in town, or there is a big possibility that they will come to our home."

I had only been in the country a few days, but the only option I had now was to leave Somalia. We all agreed. "Where could I go?" I asked. "An English-speaking country would be my first choice. What about America or Canada? Are those countries a possibility? What if I seek asylum in the US?"

I was desperate to find an alternative to South Africa. Going back there would be a failure and would shatter the hopes of my family for a better life. "I would go to the US if that was possible."

"I understand why you want to do that," Fawzia said. "If you can take that dangerous trip and are committed to it, we will support your decision." She did not ask her husband, just looking at him, and he nodded. Then Omar told me they had recently sold a farm and so now had the money that would take care of the people smugglers' fees.

Omar and my sister together made a plan for the remaining time and a method for how I would hide inside the house. And should someone, even a neighbor, come to the door, which one of us should open it. My task was to hide. They would tell anyone who asked that I had left and wouldn't be coming back, and they didn't know where I went. All this was for their safety and mine.

"So if we are not here," my sister said, "the last one to leave will lock the door. You must not open it, and you must remain in the house unless going back to the washrooms. At all times, you must be very, very vigilant."

*****

That evening, the same red sedan came to Fawzia's home. I was hiding but able to see them drive up. Two masked men got out of the car with rifles. I kept myself hidden while Fawzia answered a pound on the door. She stood in the doorway and waited.

"Where is Ahmed?" I heard one of them say. "He has received the letter today. He knows what to do."

"He is not here," she answered. "What do you want with him? His money will not even come to him for two days."

"Ahmed must leave Somalia in twenty-four hours, or he will face the consequences." Without waiting for a response, they returned to the car and drove off.

*****

The following day, I went to the police station. The police told me they had limited resources and that killings by the terrorist group were common, so it would be in my best interest to leave the country if I had the means. One police officer said, "You should just ignore them, but for your safety, you should at least leave Jowhar." He made it clear they could not help me. All they could do was give me friendly advice, which was, of course, no help at all.

I knew I could not just leave Jowhar and stay somewhere else in Somalia because Al-Shabaab controls large parts of the country. They would track me down. Besides that, I was a member of the Ashraf clan, a minority. *Who would risk taking me in?*

After that, I returned to my sister's house. It was noon.

My auntie sold a cow to help Omar because he alone could not raise all the money I needed for my journey to the US. Omar gave me some of the money, but most went to the people smuggler he was dealing with in Mogadishu, whom he knew. That night, I would not sleep. I had to leave that evening before sunset to satisfy Al-Shabaab's timetable.

For more on Al-Shabaab, its history, and atrocities, see "Appendix A: Al-Shabaab."

2

Escape

> Life begins at the edge of your fears.
>
> —Matshona Dhliwayo

Ahmed

March 29, 2016—Jowhar, Somalia

Jowhar is divided by the river Shebelle. On the eastern side is a house on the outskirts of town. I went there in the dark the night I was leaving Somalia. That house is where a car came to pick me up.

From Jowhar to Mogadishu is about ninety kilometers. The roads are very rough, and the shortest route is the worst route because there are a few places along it where Al-Shabaab hides. We had to use an alternative way, a much-longer route that goes near the sea. It was called an illegal road because the militias who guarded it collected tolls. If you paid ten dollars from Jowhar to Mogadishu using the short way, you would pay forty dollars for the illegal road. But it was the safest way since Al-Shabaab stayed clear of it.

I squeezed into a compact car with Omar and three other guys. Nobody knew the next person's story because you could trust no one. There were informants, so everyone kept a low profile. We left Jowhar at midnight for Mogadishu and arrived before sunrise.

Omar had been in contact with a few smugglers from Mogadishu. He had taken my picture and sent it to one of them via WhatsApp. The smugglers had organized a travel document, a Somalian passport, which I knew would be fake. There was no way they could arrange it in such a short space of time—they took no fingerprints, and I filled out no forms. By then, I was more than happy to do anything. I only wanted to get out of Somalia.

We were to meet the smuggler at a restaurant around eight o'clock. Omar introduced me to a middle-aged man who was waiting in a good-looking car. "This is the man—he will remain nameless—who will take you as far as Panama," Omar said.

The smuggler looked at me for a minute. He seemed to be sizing me up. "Guys like you shouldn't be returning to Somalia," he said. "You should have sought advice and listened to the elders before you returned. Somalia is not what you see in the newspaper. This is the reality, and now you see it with your own eyes. I hope you will tell guys like you when you see them."

"I promise you, sir," I said. "I will."

With so many people in our group and my constant looking around nervously to see if we were all okay, it was difficult to say goodbye to Omar, but I was sad about leaving him and worried about his well-being. He had stood by my side from the beginning, right to our parting—he was an honorable man.

"Take care, Ahmed," Omar said. "We will miss you."

I shook his hand but had no words to say.

But now, it was time. The smuggler took me and the three others to the airport in his beautiful car. We were not allowed to exchange details or have conversations. He was firmly in charge. "Do not talk," he said. "Mind your own business."

Using our fake passports, we boarded an airplane. It took us from Mogadishu to Bula Hawo, Somalia, which is very close to the border with Kenya.

Because I did not have a Kenyan visa on my passport, the smuggler worked this out with a bribe to the border agents. He paid the visa fee, and I received a stamp on the passport and handed it back to the smuggler. We entered Kenya and stayed in Mandera that night.

From Mandera to Nairobi, traveling by hired car took one day and one night.

*****

I did not want to call Zoya all this time because it would cause her emotional problems. My family had their own difficulties in Johannesburg, which was getting more and more dangerous for refugees, so I called her only once I was in Nairobi. She seemed shocked at first, then saddened, but as we talked, she said she was grateful I had left Somalia and was now in a safe place. "Are you okay?" Zoya kept asking. "Are you hiding anything from me?"

"I'm okay," I said. "I don't know how I will travel or when I will get to the US, but I am taking it one step at a time. The smuggler assures me he will get me there."

"Have you been injured? Are you okay?"

"No, I was not beaten up. I was not shot. I had just left Somalia as soon as I could when Al-Shabaab threatened me. And now I'm in Nairobi. Please don't worry about me."

"You are doing the right thing, Ahmed," she said, "but the kids and I will miss you terribly. We will pray for you every day."

The smuggler put me in a house in a suburb. Six others were staying there. We could not live freely as we did not have any legal status in Kenya. The place we stayed looked set up to house people in transit. There were women and men, and they all had one thing in mind: to leave Kenya. I was told that within one month, everything would be all right. I was waiting for my turn.

During those days in Kenya, I called Zoya when I could to reassure her. This was a time of waiting.

*****

My next step was to fly out of Kenya. The smugglers had connections with the airlines and the airports. They would arrange whatever was possible. Some routes cost more, but that could not be helped. I learned that sometimes you could not choose what you wanted. You would only be given one option, and if you declined it, you had to wait for another chance. If you refused three times, the smuggler would not deal with you anymore. Then, alas, you were stuck on your own with no way to move forward.

The smuggler came to my quarters one night. "Okay, tonight you are leaving. Get ready," he said. "You must follow me. You don't talk to anyone. You follow my instruction. You will go to a specific counter at the airline. You don't say anything but just look at the agent. He already has your picture. He knows what to do."

I got dressed and put my things into a traveling bag. I was not carrying much. I had less than six sets of clothes, one pair of shoes, one pair of sandals, and a few other things.

The smuggler checked how I was dressed and then looked at me. "You shouldn't look scared," he instructed. "Pretend to be going for a meeting as a business owner or as a tourist—with confidence."

I had little choice except to cooperate. He was in charge, and I did not know what to do.

We flew at about eleven o'clock that night. It was my first overseas flight. The airplane was very noisy and packed with people. There were many Europeans. We landed and taxied at an airport in what looked like an Arab country. We walked through the airport to our next flight.

Because of my situation, I was told not to look like a stranger, not to look around, and not to look suspicious. So I was not reading signs but following this guy, like a child would do, trying to smile and pretend as if I had been traveling before.

We arrived in Panama City and went through security. Somehow, the smuggler had obtained a Panama visa stamp, either before we left or on the spot with a security agent he knew. We stayed in Panama that day and overnight.

*****

The smuggler from Somalia handed me over to another man with my passport, all my documentation, and the dollars they had previously agreed upon. All the smugglers worked together. The money Omar paid in Mogadishu applied to cover every smuggler's expense from Somalia to Mexico. They were like a chain that worked together.

The smuggler in Latin America was Hispanic. He could speak very little English, and because of the sensitivity surrounding my trip, we could not talk the way I wanted. It was only Q and A between us. I could only ask him the necessary questions as I did not know him, and he did not know me. We were more like business partners. He was only there to carry out his mission: to take me from Panama to Mexico, and that was it. He was always cautious and would give me instructions and repeat those instructions twice. Sometimes he would ask me to repeat back to him to make sure I understood. One fatal error could lead to my arrest.

We arrived back at the Panama airport. There, the smuggler told me to go to a specific window in security, and by the time I arrived there, the immigration officer already knew me. He had my details, so he just looked at me and gave me the travel document that I needed. That is how I knew my smuggler was well prepared.

*****

From Panama City, we flew to Tegucigalpa, Honduras, where we joined others, all men, being smuggled. We crossed the country by bus and sometimes on foot, especially when we needed to avoid a police control point. We would just come to a town, stay there a few hours—sometimes one day, sometimes one night—and when it was safe to do so, we would proceed. The smuggler was communicating with officials all along the way and asked me to show my documents to them.

Many times, he had to pay the police. Other times, he would say to us, "I don't have connections with anyone here, so we have to walk a little bit. Sorry, guys." And we would cooperate. He was our lifeline, so we always kept him in sight.

When we arrived at the border between Honduras and Guatemala after five days, the smuggler went to check with immigration, while we waited for two hours at the border. They let us in.

*****

Guatemala is a small country. During our travels there, we slept for two nights for five US dollars per night. On the third day, we departed by car, and it was nighttime before we arrived at a small city called Tecun Uman on the Suchiate River. This was the natural border between Guatemala and Mexico.

"I want each of you to put your hands in your pockets. Now take out the pockets and let me see what you have," the smuggler said, and we all complied with his inspection. Then he took all our documents, our passports, and any papers that could trace us back to where we came from.

"This is where my contract ends," he said. "Once you cross the river into Mexico, you will be on your own, but I have told you what to do from there. You should not experience any problems."

Traveling at night, being stripped of all my documents, and being told that I would be on my own from here, despite his assurances, made me terrified to go further. The man who had guided us, the smuggler who knew what to do, was leaving us all by ourselves.

3

Two Rivers

You are searching for something that may as yet be indefinable.
A border crosser questions the very idea of home.

—Sergio Troncoso, *Nepantla Familias*

Ahmed

May 10, 2016—Rio Suchiate

My next destination was Tapachula, Mexico. It was good that the smuggler took my documents because the Mexican authorities would know they were fake. Mexican immigration was working with the Americans, so they would automatically send any document that interested them to the US, jeopardizing the whole operation. Once in Mexico, they would take my photo and fingerprints, and the smuggler had briefed us about what would happen after that.

Ciudad Tecun Uman, Guatemala, on the banks of Rio Suchiate, is well-known among immigrants who want to cross into Mexico. Undocumented immigrants do not take the bridge with its immigration and customs guards posted at each end but take one of the many improvised rafts or boats available for hire. On some days of the year, the river is shallow, and a person can wade across. But now, it was deep in the middle, so we had to go by boat. The boat owner had an accomplice, who drove each of us one by one into the river by bicycle, and once all were aboard, we started across.

While we were in the middle of the river, the ferry owner demanded more money, but my dollars were getting short. I had to save all I could to get across Mexico.

It was nighttime, but I could tell that we were about, I will say, fifteen people, mainly from Asia, a few from Haiti, and we had some other African men. They were speaking English and French to each other, but only one had Spanish. I decided not to talk, just to sit quietly while they argued.

We had agreed to pay five dollars each, but now they wanted fifteen. Speaking for the others, one person told our interpreter, "We can't pay more, you know, so tell him just to take us back." After a long negotiation in Spanish, the ferryman agreed we did not have to come up with any more money, so he took us the rest of the way. It was around ten o'clock that evening.

Some men and boys were waiting for us on the other side of the river, at the river's edge, in the small town of Hidalgo, Mexico. Waving their hands, they motioned for us to come with them.

"They say they will help us," our interpreter said. "They say, 'We will take you to a hotel. We know where you people are going.'"

But when I looked at them, I felt I could not trust them. They were not wearing their sandals but had them in their hands, which was a sign that they wanted to speed up. They wanted to rip us off and run. I did not want to gamble, so I went solo. I took a shortcut and went straight to a hotel.

When I entered the hotel, there was a couple, a man and his wife, who were running the place, and they charged me twenty-five dollars. I did not eat any food. I was so worried. The sweat was dripping from me as I tried to sleep. Finally, I slept but not very well. What I had heard about Mexico and all the cartels was in the back of my mind, and it bothered me I no longer had a smuggler to direct my next steps.

*****

Early in the morning, I took a minibus that was headed to Tapachula. Once in town, my intention was to take a taxi to the immigration center and tell them I wanted to request asylum in the US. I knew from the smuggler that the Mexican government would detain me for a few days and then warn me I had fifteen days to leave the country. Then I would be free to travel north to the border with the US.

The Spanish folks on the bus seemed to know each other. I got the feeling that they had been on this route before. But when the bus had traveled only ten minutes, it stopped at an immigration roadblock. They arrested me there, and I was not alone. Only a few of those cleared got back on the bus, those who had national ID cards.

The Mexican immigration police took the rest of us in a van to the immigration center. The large building was busy and crowded. It held around fifteen hundred people already.

They screened me to ensure that the police did not want me because of a criminal record, and because I said I was headed to the US, I was taken next to an office for US immigration. An American who could speak the Somali language took my photo and fingerprints. When they learned I could speak English, they interviewed me two or three times, and when I thought there were no more interviews, another group of American officers asked me the same questions.

Next, even though I was in Mexico, two agents from the American FBI interrogated me. One asked me many questions. The other agent was not saying anything. He just watched me and took notes. They wanted to know everything about me—my name, where I came from, how I was traveling, and what made me leave my country—but by this time, I felt I had nothing to hide, and I felt everything went well.

There were seven other Somalis. Some could speak English, but said, "No English," to avoid a lot of questions being asked.

I was honest and confident. "You know, I can speak English," I said. I wanted to cooperate fully. Their questions did not bother me.

Before my arrival, people used to stay in detention there for one or two months. There was an immigrant from Guatemala who could not take the stress level and, as a result, took his own life. After that, the officials were told not to keep detainees for over two weeks unless there was some serious reason that they had to stay longer.

I stayed there for five days and four nights. I was supposed to be released earlier, but because other Somalis could not speak English, immigration kept me there so I could interpret for them, which I did not mind. Finally, they released me from the detention center with a letter that said I had fifteen days to leave Mexico. That document allowed me enough time to travel from where I was, near Mexico's southern border with Guatemala, to the border with the US.

*****

Now, I had to prepare for my trip to the US border. Mexico is a huge country, so I aimed to go to the nearest border crossing, a place called Reynosa. Traveling by road is very dangerous, I was told, because of the cartel, and it is easy to be recognized as an immigrant, as a target. So I sold my phone, which I had hidden all this time in my shoes. I now had some traveling money, which was easier to hide.

Other immigrants told me that the cartel would easily rob you. Sometimes, if you wore fine clothes and had identity papers, they would hijack you to demand a ransom. Other times, they might force you to carry drugs into the US. The possibilities of whatever they might do to you made the journey by road hazardous.

After they released me from the detention center and I came to Tapachula, I met two Somalian men. They were in a similar situation to me, having little money. We decided to stick together for mutual protection. "Well, the three of us, why don't we hire one hotel?" one of them said.

To save money, we found a hotel with a queen bed where the three of us slept, and we traveled together and ate only once or twice a day.

Tapachula was filled with migrants. People would gather all the documents and forms that they needed. Some would have haircuts. Others would say, "Well, I want to eat ice cream because I cannot later. I will be in jail."

There were a lot of mixed emotions. I could see everyone was sad and stressed, not knowing what to expect.

Because we feared the cartel, who controlled a large portion of Mexico, it was safer to fly and go by bus once we landed in the northern part of the country. We had to make an important decision: claim asylum in Texas, where I wanted to go, or possibly California.

There were a lot of trail advisors. People would make many phone calls to the US to find out the conditions of one place or another. In Texas, they would normally detain people for less than six months. That is what we were told, at least. In California, the authorities held some people for as long as one year and eight months. We did not want to stay long in detention, even though California might be better in some other ways, so the three of us decided we would cross the border to Texas.

*****

My Somalian traveling companions and I had lots of time to discuss our plans as we had to wait around for five days to get seats on a flight north.

We flew to Mexico City and from there, Monterrey, Mexico. From the airport, we traveled by bus for almost three hours until we came to Reynosa. Then we had to take a taxi through the city to the US border. We were told that we could not trust all the taxis. Some of the taxis were fake, run by the cartel, so we had to double-check for a registered taxi, and once we found one, we took it to the US border, which was not far, about twenty minutes.

At the border, from across the Rio Grande, we saw a giant American flag. Stretching out before it on the bridge was a long queue, so we knew that, yes, this was the US border. There were sighs of relief, and our hopes revived. We had made the long journey.

You could see the joy. You could see the smiles, but the cheerful mood was mixed with fear of what would come next. One guy I was traveling with was young. He was an orphan—terrorists had killed his father in Somalia—but he had a quick smile. He was the youngest, by far the youngest of us, I would say around twenty.

Together, we walked across the Rio Grande and into the immigration center. One by one, each of us requested asylum.

4

Land of the Free

Hope meets you halfway on a bridge called faith.

—Bryant H. McGill

Ahmed

May 23, 2016—McAllen, Texas

Around one o'clock, our little group of Somalis entered the immigration center at the border. An officer came straight to us and took us aside. He seemed well-experienced and professional. It felt like he had been expecting us. He knew where we came from and what we looked like because he had our papers and pictures from the US offices in Mexico.

We went to a private room, where he interviewed us, and another officer took notes. They knew who could speak English and who could not, which helped me big-time. One officer was kind. He brought us burgers and listened carefully to us. They kept us there overnight.

The following morning, a bus took us to a much-larger immigration center, the US Border Patrol station in McAllen, Texas. We traveled for about an hour and passed by an airport. The immigration center was an excellent facility. There were many people, immigrants from all over the world. They kept us there for twenty-nine days until immigration officials could find a longer-term place somewhere in the US where the government would detain us until they decided our individual asylum cases. Where that would be was not up to us.

*****

On a Wednesday, right after midnight, the security guard started calling out names just as I was falling asleep. My name and two Somali companions' names were called, as well as many others.

A guard escorted me from my cell into another room, a very tiny room. There were so many small rooms. Each room hosted five to seven men with one toilet inside. And they kept us there until five o'clock in the morning. They handcuffed each of us with a chain to our waist. Our ankles were chained to our waist as well. Then they transported us by bus a short distance to the airport. People from outside could not see us because the bus windows were tinted, but we had no trouble seeing anyone outside.

When we arrived at the airport, we entered from a particular place designated for immigrants. We were all in a line. We numbered thirty-five, all of us men. Early on, they had separated the women from the men, and except for three Somalis, the others were from countries in Latin America.

We boarded an airplane with propellers. It was noisy, dull gray, and military style. We were still in chains, our hands and feet tied to our waists. Before we took off, the flight attendant announced, "In the event that something goes wrong while we are in the air, you should grab the parachute." He displayed how we were to use it to survive.

How could I grab the parachute, I thought, *if my waist, legs, and hands were chained together?* I could not even hold a cup of water. None of us could eat the food he gave us. I soon realized he was following procedure and did not really care about us.

We were on the plane for five hours. I was miserable, thirsty, and hungry. All I could do was peek out the window. As we descended, I could see fields and roads, and then a large city came into view.

Everything looked very clean. When we finally landed and I was told the place's name, it was still unknown to me because I had never heard of Iowa. I had never heard of Arabella.

About seven cars were waiting for us, and again, all the windows were tinted. They divided us into groups. Two officials from ICE (Immigration and Customs Enforcement) escorted all of us. One of them sat in our car in front next to the driver, and we were sitting in the second and third rows behind a divider.

I was excited and hoped that maybe after one month, I would be one of those people I imagined walking in the streets, getting a job, and driving a car. And I was dreaming, not knowing that when I came to Arabella, they would keep me in jail for a very long time.

Unfortunately, my traveling friends did not come with me. They split us up and took them in a different car somewhere else. And to this day, I do not know where they are.

*****

June 21, 2016—Arabella, Iowa

After I arrived at Meadows County Corrections (MCC), I had to fill out some forms. They bagged my belongings and all my clothes and gave me an orange jumpsuit to wear. I met an officer with a mustache. I will not forget him. He was not friendly because he gave me the wrong size. I asked for a medium, but he gave me an extralarge. And when I told him that, you know, these clothes do not fit me properly, they're bigger than me, he used some words I could not repeat. And he told me to go back to where I came from.

When I received those prison clothes, it broke my heart. In Texas, we had good-looking blue shirts and pants and actual shoes. Here, they gave us one-piece orange clothes and some soft orange plastic shoes with holes. You could buy approved sneakers if you could afford them, but I had little money and needed to save.

"Well, I'm not a criminal even though I look like one," I said to myself, and I expected to be treated well. Yet I could say nothing to them, even politely, to disagree.

The guards would say, "Hey, you don't have any choice. You just do what we tell you," and that was said in an unfriendly way. So many of the guards and officers were insulting.

Texas detention was where I could walk outside, get some fresh air, and play sports, and they treated me well. But this place was completely different compared to Texas. Meadows County Jail was very dark, very gloomy. I could see sorrowful faces everywhere I looked.

They took me to K-mod, which held forty-two guys in twenty-one two-person cells. K-mod was maximum security—no sun, no activity. I realized I was in trouble; I was really, really in trouble. I had never been to a jail or prison, never been to a two-man cell. Most of these guys would be on the news or in the newspaper because they had committed a crime. I was terrified.

The next fifty-five days of maximum security were the longest days of my life. And I did not know why I was put in K-Mod; I never had a clear explanation. Either it was because there was no other place to put me—the jail was full—or it was where they put newcomers to show them the harsh realities of jail, to make released prisoners think twice before committing another crime.

As I entered K-mod, the first person I saw was a guy from South Sudan called Kazeem. I started talking with him and asked him many questions, even though I didn't know him. I needed to speak with someone, anyone. I was so upset. Nothing had prepared me for this. I had not realized that my life could change so drastically in only a few hours.

I started out sharing a cell, not with a criminal or gang member but luckily with an immigrant who was on the same flight from Texas. He was from Guatemala and couldn't speak English, and my Spanish was terrible. I only started to learn Spanish when I was in Texas, so we had very little ability to communicate. But what was important was not the words. We shared a common experience, and the sadness on our faces was a far bigger reality, a language, in itself. Even without words, we could understand each other.

When first I could, I took a shower, but I left my soap in the washroom, and I did not know someone else would take it if you forgot. When I reached my cell, I realized my mistake. I hurried back within two minutes, but my soap was gone, and I was told this would happen because it was an opportunity for someone, so I learned always to keep my stuff in a safe place.

The first meal I received was terrible, full of water with no taste. It was food that was not cooked with good intentions, with very little nutrition or protein. Although it made me upset, I had no choice but to eat it and try to enjoy it.

Some cells were allocated based on one of two gang groups, the Bloods and the Crips, who were well-known in Arabella. They separated them from the others, and every gang member was sticking to his gang.

The air had a stale smell, and the halls were very narrow. We didn't have a place to walk to get some exercise. We were always under electric lights because the small windows were few. We did not see the sun. I could not tell if it was day or night, except for the time and daily routine, and it was a very sad situation. I never expected to see myself in a place like that.

Most of the security guards could have been more friendly and in a better mood, but they were happy to be in a position of authority, and they controlled us. Every day I would see a fight over some minor thing because the prisoners always seemed frustrated. The long wait for court dates irritated everybody. Some of them had been there for eight months, nine months. Some of them would be convicted and go to long-term prison.

One of my cellmates, not the guy from Guatemala, had made bail. A short time later, he was on the news. He knocked down an older woman and stole her purse. The incident happened in a church somewhere in Arabella, and his face was caught on the security camera. His picture was in the newspaper. Most of the guys in K-mod were on the news after they were released. I could see them on TV. Because I knew them and shared a cell with some of them, I started asking myself, "What did I do? Why did I deserve to be in this place? Is this what America was all about? Is this how immigrants were being treated?"

*****

The first time I called Zoya from Meadows County Jail, I was happy to hear her voice. But I tried not to say anything about what I had experienced, which would be difficult for her to hear because I knew she was alone and with the kids. If she knew I had a tough time, it would put her under much stress—living as a single mom in South Africa, you know, taking care of our kids without me—so I tried to paint a different picture and focus on the future, that everything would work out and would one day be okay. "I will be released soon, so you don't have to worry," I said. "Now I'm in the US, and that is the most important."

But deep down in my heart, it was a different story when I hung up the phone. The days were long, the hours were long, the minutes were long, and I could not sleep at night the way I wanted to because of worry.

*****

One day, at the infirmary, the nurse took an X-ray, and I was told I had something on my chest, so they had to take me to a county hospital to do a CT scan. Two officers transported me. When we reached the hospital, they put me in a wheelchair. Because it was a public place—and the public does not really like to see a man being chained, especially someone walking with chains on their ankles—it would disturb them, spoil their day because here was this hardcore criminal. So here in the wheelchair, I was told to act sick, you know, and they had to push me, even though I was very fit. I had to play their game.

When they provided the wheelchair, it was like, "Well, now we did *our* part. Now you do *your* part. You pretend you are sick." But when someone is being pushed in a wheelchair, they are invisible. People do not look at them closely.

All the time, there was a pattern of secrecy. When they transported prisoners, they did it at night or behind tinted glass. They had shirts with the ICE name, but they always wore a jacket on top, so people did not know. Only when they came to the jail, they would remove the jacket. When they went out, they put the jacket back on so they looked like ordinary people.

*****

In the jail, the laundry was the biggest transporter of communication. If two people who had been arrested for the same crime but could not communicate with one another but wanted to discuss their case, they would use the laundry to send notes back and forth. If it was like weed, cigarettes, or any drug that came from outside the jail, it came to an inmate through the laundry.

It happened like this: they gave every inmate a unique laundry number, so if you wanted something sent, you put your note with your clothes in your bag. When it went to the laundry, the workers took nothing out at first. The bag had strings and holes, so the letters and clothes were washed together, dried together. In the sorting of bags, laundry workers moved the messages and other stuff between the bags. Then the inmate came to the laundry, gave his bag number, and collected it.

Inmates first made agreements with the laundry workers, who were fellow inmates, about how often they wanted the service—once only, weekly, or monthly—and then agreed on how much the commission would be. You never paid for this service by sending cash through the laundry. Payment happened in one of two ways. If you had someone outside the jail, you gave the number of the inmate to them, and they put money into his account. The other method was if the laundry worker needed items from the commissary, you bought them and gave them to him when you picked up your laundry.

The money put in an inmate's account depended on the kind of service. For example, we had guys who bought weed for one dollar per cigarette and sold each for five dollars. Then they had the money to buy more the following week. They were in business. Some of the security guards and some nurses were part of this scheme.

The nurses were not under suspicion, so a few would bring the weed, and their things would not be checked. So an inmate would say he was sick, and he made sure it was the day that the nurse who had the weed was working. Once he saw the nurse, he would get the stuff and then go to the washroom and put it under his clothes. When he came back to his cell, that was it. Sometimes the nurse would give the stuff to the laundry people, who would deliver it to the inmate.

Having been around all the guys in jail, I heard about all these deals. It was a big subject of conversation. If an inmate wanted to do something, there was always a way to get it done.

*****

I applied to become a *trustee*, and because I had a good jail record, followed all the jail rules, and got along with others, they accepted me. It was a measure of respect. I came to the other side of the jail, where I was put in cellblock, Mod-3. And I started wearing white clothes, getting a bit more food, a little more freedom, separate toilets, and a shower.

It was in Mod-3 that I met Kumar, a Somali refugee, like me. He told me he had already been in jail for eleven months. My heart, which had almost mended, was broken again. I stood with him and asked, "Have you really been here for eleven months?" I was not ready for his answer. I was not prepared to stay in jail for that long because Zoya and the kids were waiting for me.

5

Meadows County Corrections

> Look down! Look down!
> They've all forgotten you.
>
> —Claude-Michel Schönberg, *Les Misérables* (1987 play)

Annie

If someone asked me how I got started visiting immigrant detainees, I would say it is a long story, but three life experiences would stand out most for me. I grew up on a farm with many sisters and brothers. Of all the kids there, I was the one most attracted to the underdog, the sick animal, or the animal nobody wanted: the ill bunny, the stray dog—whatever. I wanted that one. And it didn't matter if the cat died, the bunny died, or some other animal had to be put down. That was the one I chose for however long it lived.

And it wasn't only animals. When I heard about people in trouble, my heart went out to them. I was probably the only kid in grade school who, when they said it was a good thing to pray for the most forgotten soul in purgatory, I would pray for the most forgotten soul in prison.

After my marriage to Michael, we adopted two mentally disabled children, and I became a foster mom for kids needing a home while something was resolved in their families. It was good training in how to listen with my heart. One foster child, age six, knew his rights. The first time I met him, he told me, "I is a foster child, and you can't hurt me."

I lowered myself to his level and looked him in the eyes. "Oh, Billy, nobody is going to hurt you. You are safe here with us. You are safe now."

Another boy of about seven would, without words, sit on the floor, cry tears of fear and shame, and bang his head on the wall if he thought he had done something wrong. It took many months of reassurance that he was a good kid, just like the other kids in our home. Miko stayed with us for a year until his mother got a job and was free of an abusive boyfriend. I will never forget Miko.

Once our kids grew up, I went with Michael to Uganda, East Africa. For a couple of years, I worked with people who had endured the IDP (internally displaced person) camps and the atrocities that came with twenty years of civil war. It was a *sea of need*, this place, and you could drown in that sea. But my desires, faith, and training took me to an understanding of the strength of the people: their coping skills, survival skills—a people who had endured despite everything. They were a great inspiration to me.

All those skills would come into play, and all those desires and training were invaluable as I began visiting detainees at our local jail.

*****

I drove downtown to the Meadows County Corrections, a jail where they held people charged with crimes waiting for court dates but could not make bail. But a few immigrants were also in detention. Most were innocent of any crime—they were seeking asylum. The nonprofit of which I was a new member had assigned me to one of them.

A guard ushered me upstairs to a small visiting room. I sat and waited. Soon, a detainee entered through a different door. The young man sat, leaned back in his chair, and looked at me directly in my eyes. His appearance distracted me. His hair was frizzy and curly. He reminded me of my sweet nephew, an Asian-Caucasian blend, who was just as lovely as can be.

"My name is Annie," I said and added what I always say, "Do you know who I am?"

"No," he said.

"I'm from AIDVP, the Arabella Immigrant Detainee Visitor Program." And I waited for him to say, "Oh, what does that mean?" But that is not what he said.

He sat back, glared at me, and crossed his arms. "I know who you really are," he said.

What? I couldn't believe my ears.

"I know who you really are. You're an agent from One World Order, and they sent you here to interrogate me."

What the hell is One World Order? But my face was not moving. I just looked at him calmly, trying to show compassion and interest and no shock, nothing to upset him, because I was curious about this. "I don't know what you mean," I said.

"You're from One World Order, and you're here to interrogate me, and it's not going to happen. You're not going to get anything out of me, and you can just turn around and leave now," he said.

"Well, yeah, I can, but I want you to know that nobody sent me. Nobody sent me. I'm just a volunteer."

"Don't. Don't try to get out of it. I know who you are. You can just put down the show. It's over. I'm on to you."

He kept repeating this in different ways while rocking back and forth in his chair. He watched me with a smirk, not so much like he was a real bad guy coming to get me because if he had done that, I would have called the guard to the door. It was more like he had caught a mouse in this little room, and he was going to let me know he knew what the jig was.

"I don't know what you are talking about," I said. "Even though you think you're sure about who I am, I can tell you that, in this room, you have all the power. I did not come here to get power over you or to make something happen to you. If you say, 'I never want to see you again, Annie,' believe me, I will not come back! I am a volunteer. I drove for a half hour to get here just to see you. And if you say, 'I never want you to come back,' that's what's going to happen."

For some reason, maybe it was the emotion in my voice, he seemed to believe me. He sat back with a little more of a puzzle on his face then straightened up again. "All right, this is what you do. You're being manipulated, and you don't know it, so whoever sent you, this AIDVP or whoever, they're not who you think they are. So you go back and you tell them, but very nicely so they don't get upset with you. You just tell them, 'I don't want to be in this organization anymore,' and quietly back out of it. Just get out of it. You don't know what you're in, okay?"

"Okay. I can leave now, and nobody will bother you again." I was not getting through to him, and he firmly believed what he was saying. The guard came to our conference room after I knocked on the door.

The man with curly hair walked out ahead of me and kept walking down the hall. The guard turned to me and said, "That was a short one."

I rolled my eyes. "Yes, it was." I figured I was not the first to hear of his conspiracy theories. I imagined this guy not functioning in jail without everybody knowing his beliefs, so we left it at that, and I never saw him again.

*****

September 12, 2016—Arabella, Iowa

It was a Monday in mid-September. My appointment was for 1:00 p.m. to visit Ahmed, an asylum seeker from Somalia. His name and, more importantly, his inmate number for identifying him in the jail, AIDVP had assigned to me.

Although I am a certified spiritual director (not a counselor) with a degree in communication, I was apprehensive. This was my first time meeting him. I wondered what he would be like. Would he trust me? He had agreed to the visit. That was a start. I had been a little jaded from my visit with the conspiracy fellow.

As I pulled into the parking lot for visitors to the jail, I went over what I would say to tell him why I was there and anything else I could say that would help break the ice. When I walked into the building, I put my phone, keys, purse, and everything that was in my pockets into a locker and kept the locker key and my ID. The jailor also allowed me a small notebook and pencil. Next was a walk through the X-ray booth and check-in at the desk. I showed the guard my ID and told him about my organization and whom I was visiting. Then I took a trip up an elevator to a glass-walled anteroom. I waited until an officer looked up from his work and pressed the buzzer.

"Who are you here to see?" he asked as he buzzed me in.

"Ahmed, MCC number 24601-01."

He directed me to visiting room 5. Inside was a light switch, a concrete table, and two plastic chairs. When I pushed through the heavy glass door, I propped it open with my foot. The doorknob wouldn't work from inside. And I wanted the guard to see me down the hall from his vantage point near the elevator and remember I was there.

I had no guarantee that the visit would begin on time, but if the inmate delayed his coming, the guard promised me a full hour for our conversation. Today, a disturbance caused a lockdown, and everyone waited. Jail time was slow compared to the outside world. Nothing in the jail was urgent, and no appointments were that important. We must follow the rules and procedures no matter how long they might take. Inmates and guards were the moving parts in this machine, which ground out the days and nights.

They had to bring inmates down a separate elevator, hallway, and a different door to our little room. Like every other inmate, he wore an orange jumpsuit and matching orange clogs. But on top of the orange jail garb, he was wearing a white garment that seemed to set him apart. I learned later that he was a trustee with some extra privileges. As he entered quietly, he bent his head forward. He was looking down, not meeting my eyes. He kept looking down when he sat at the table and faced me. There was a pause as he waited for me to speak first.

"Do you know who I am?" I asked. "My name is Annie. I'm from the AIDVP program. I'm a volunteer, not a lawyer, not clergy. I've just come as a friend, someone you can talk to. Anything you say to me is confidential. I'm somebody who will listen to you. I can come every week if you want me to, but you don't have to see me. You have all the power. If you say, 'I don't want to see that lady ever again,' you won't." Finished with my introductory spiel, I waited for his reply.

I will always remember his response. He slowly looked up, down again, and straight ahead at me. His eyes were swimming with tears. "You don't know me, and you came to see me," he said. "I wish for you…that you could spend one day, just one day, locked in this place. Then you would know what you have done for me. I haven't spoken to anyone since I got here." His voice was heavy with loneliness and isolation. "I don't know how to thank you," he said. "I have nothing to give."

I was taken aback by the powerful emotion of the moment: the vulnerability, the dignity, and the bruised strength of this survivor. The silence held so much unsaid.

"What is your name?" I asked as my words caught in my throat. I never expected this.

"They call me Mahamed." I knew that was his middle name. He must have kept his first name hidden from the inmates and guards, a bit of privacy in a place where everything was under observation.

"Mahamed," I said. "You do have something to give. It's precious. I would be honored if you would share it with me. Please… tell me your story."

And he did. He told me the familiar tale of asylum seekers: war, terror, and loss; love and separation; abandonment and hope; plans made and lost. A chaotic mix of suffering, triumph, humiliation, empowerment, and running for your life—all the twists and turns of a modern-day exodus. He was honest and long in the telling.

At last, he paused, and the quiet deepened. "Do you have a lawyer?" I asked.

"I don't have any legal representation or family members that are willing to assist," Ahmed said.

We continued to meet every week whenever possible. Over that time, the jail visiting room, that vessel for conversation, became a holy place. He was so gracious and candid. Receiving his story was one of my life's most graced and transformational experiences.

6

Befriended

A real friend is one who walks in when
the rest of the world walks out.

—Walter Winchell

Annie

That evening, while our first visit was still fresh in my mind, I wrote a letter to Ahmed. I included one of my homemade cards—a strong, uplifting message (usually a famous quote) matched with an appropriate picture that I had downloaded from a stock image website—a little something that might inspire and cheer him.

September 12, 2016
Hello Ahmed,

It was lovely meeting you today. Thank you so very much for the beginnings of your amazing story. I will be blessed to hear more about your journey, your family, your dreams, and your hopes for the future.

As promised, I have enclosed an intake form for the Pro Bono (no cost) Detainee Project to potentially get you a lawyer. On the form…
- Pg 1: The intake date is when you send off the form
- By the number of people in your household, put a note saying which country they are in
- 3a asks if anyone in your home receives money because you are poor

Tell the truth about everything.

I suggest that, on the blank lines and pages, you describe when and why you had to leave Somalia, Ethiopia, South Africa, and Somalia again…much like you described to me. Also, describe what you are asking for; for example: I have no lawyer. I'd like to get a lawyer to help me…(fill in the blank).

I really look forward to seeing you again on Monday, September 26. If you have any questions about the form, we can talk about them. After Sept 26, I will not be able to visit for a month, but I will continue to send picture cards with a short message in my absence.

I am so very sorry for your troubles. I am also very impressed by your strength, courage, skills, desire to work and learn, and excellent English. You are one amazing fellow.

Know I am praying for you,
Annie

TIMOTHY LEACOCK

September 21, 2016
Hello Ahmed,

    Your friend, Kumar, [whom I had visited in jail], told me that you were not permitted to receive my letter with the Intake Form for getting a free (pro bono) lawyer. I do not know why this is. Others have mailed this form with no problem. Oh well.

    I called the organization that provides the services and form. They said the jail has the form there. You need to ask for it. It's the "Pro Bono Detainee Project Intake form." Make sure you get the pro bono Attorney form for Detainees or Immigration, as there may be several kinds. I don't know whom you ask or if you must *fly a kite* [make a written request].

    The person also said the [Arabella Justice for Immigrants (AJFI)] organization regularly holds information sessions/workshops about pro bono work at the jail. So, watch for any announcements about this and sign up if they are offered.

    If you can tell me your sizes (shirt, slacks, shoes) when I visit next, that would be helpful.

    I look forward to seeing you next Tuesday (date change from Monday as requested by the jail).

Peace,
Annie

*****

    After returning from my California trip to see family, I had another visit with Ahmed. Rather than talk about jail troubles, I leaned into the positive. "You told me a little about being a trustee.

You have special privileges, like moving around more freely and wearing better clothing. What are some other things that you enjoy about being a trustee?"

"The cells of the trustees are located in a better part of the jail," Ahmed said, "so the toilets and showers are now far from us, not in the cell, which is a big deal. We are allowed to move around until eleven o'clock at night. Other inmates are locked up at nine o'clock. The trustees can play a little game of cards or sit together in one bed and just talk for two or three hours.

"Everyone talks about his life or, you know, something that's inspiring. Basically, it feels like we are brothers. You could freely say that. I mean, we know one another, our characters, because we have a lot of time together, which other inmates don't have."

Our meeting was pleasant, and I got to know Ahmed quite well. The desire was growing in me to help him in any way I could. On top of my list was getting him a lawyer. Ahmed had been waiting to hear about getting a lawyer for over a month. I was wondering if a private attorney might provide the needed representation. I wanted Ahmed's case to succeed.

> October 27, 2016
> Hello Ahmed,
>
> It was very good meeting with you on Tuesday. The courage and patience of so many of the detainees, like you, are an inspiration to me.
>
> I connected with someone from Lutheran Family Services. Their organization—the main one here in Arabella—would provide assistance if/when you get out of jail. You call them to make an appointment to speak with a caseworker after you are released. I believe they help immigrants, refugees, and asylees get legal identification, find a place to live, obtain simple home furnishings, and get an entry-level job. They would try to find you a sponsor.

I'm trying to read up on—and understand—the US government process for getting permission to work in the USA. I know an EAD (Employment Authorization Document) provides temporary employment authorization and is the same as a work permit. How soon you can apply depends on your status. An EAD is generally good for one year, and one starts to renew it after about nine months.

I also re-connected with AJFI, and the woman in charge confirmed that once out of jail, you can call and make an appointment for a consultation with a lawyer there.

Peace,
Annie

I felt like we were getting nowhere. Getting help from a local organization depended on Ahmed's being out of jail. But how to accomplish that was the immediate question.

*****

A few weeks later, I emailed Warren Jackson, an immigration attorney in Arabella. I got his name from AIDVP. They were interested in asking him to come and speak to the group and asked if I would set it up. He came highly rated, and I wondered if he would be an excellent choice to represent Ahmed.

Emails: November 15–22, 2016
Subject: Taking on a client?

[Annie to Warren]

The best day for AIDVP to meet with you is Tuesday, Dec 6, at 7:30 AM at your office. I have asked them to email me their questions ahead of time so that I can send them to you before the meeting.

Warren, what is the fee for an hour of your time? We really appreciate your educating us for ministry!

[Warren to Annie]

That sounds good to me; I will have to be done by 8:30 A.M. to be at court before 9:00 A.M. I'm not going to charge you, either. You do great work, and I'm happy to provide any insight I can.

[Annie to Warren]

Thank you so very much, Warren!

I have been visiting a Somalian detainee seeking asylum from Al-Shabaab and other nasty dudes (he has a gunshot wound to prove it). The judge told him he had a good case (whatever that means), and he was offered bond but didn't take it because he had no money. Anyway, he's a brilliant guy, very articulate in English. Hard worker. He has no lawyer. His court case is coming up here in Arabella on Dec 6 at 1:00. I'm interested in retaining you—if you'd consider taking his case and being there for him on Dec 6.

Could we talk about this? I know the chances of a positive outcome go way up when an individual has representation. But I am superbly clueless as to what this would involve financially. I'd appreciate a call.

Thanks a million for considering!

[Warren to Annie]

Do you know what his criminal history consists of? Is his hearing on 12/6 his final one, known as an individual hearing? Did he already file an asylum application on his own (pro se)? I usually charge $5000 for these cases, but it depends on what stage of the case he's in. I'm happy to meet with him as well.

[Annie to Warren]

I do not believe there is a criminal history. He had none back in Africa. Ahmed turned himself in at the US border after the usual horrendous journey via smugglers. He was fingerprinted and photographed along this journey before reaching the USA. Ahmed says he has a clear record, but he wonders about the papers the smugglers used to get him across borders before the USA. He had no control over documents not supplied by him. Smugglers keep and control all the papers so they cannot be prosecuted.

I believe Ahmed filed for asylum himself on approximately Sept 7, 2016. A judge told him—I think the first one he saw—that he had a good case and he was offered bond. He believes the Arabella judge will make the up or down decision on December 6. Here is additional info:

Ahmed Mahamed Absame; A 789 456 701; MCC #24601-01.

Perhaps it would be best if you saw him once to size up his case. You probably need info on him to estimate costs, and Michael and I need the information to decide if we can get someone to help with the fee. I can likely find a way to put up bond if it isn't too high.

[Warren to Annie]

His hearing is on 12/6/16, and it is the final one. Normally, all documents must be submitted 15 days before that or by 11/21, but they would probably make an exception if he gets an attorney last minute. Do you think he has any supporting documentation regarding the threats?

Do you also know what his bond amount was?

[Annie to Warren]

Ahmed said he was offered bond between $1,000 and $3,000. But apparently, there is no record of that in the documentation. However much it was, he couldn't pay it. In addition to being penniless, I am told, detainees regularly refuse bond, believing that even if they could find a means of taking care of themselves outside, being out on bond considerably delays one's court hearing date.

Blessings on your conversation tomorrow.

[Warren to Annie]

I met with Ahmed on Friday. I certainly understand why you care about him. He speaks very highly of you as well! He told me he filed his asylum application instead of asking for bond. I told him that I could try to ask for bond now, but he wants to get a quick resolution on his case and go forward with his trial on 12/6. I'm happy to help him, but I will have to get everything filed ASAP as normally everything needs to be filed 15 days before, which would be tomorrow. I can probably get the judge to excuse it as he hasn't had an attorney, and he's detained, but I still need to file everything this week to play it safe with the holiday. I'm willing to represent him for $3500. Please let me know if that would be possible to arrange. Thank you!

[Annie to Warren]

Thank you so much for your efforts, Warren. Funding this amount is not out of reach. However, I need to understand a bit more.

- * What does the $3,500 cover? For example, if the prosecution contests a positive outcome, or if there is any other challenge or legal need after the 12/6 court date, do you continue to help Ahmed?

- * Do you feel Ahmed has a strong case? I know he speaks well and has a compelling story, but I don't understand what most influences a judge's decision. What has your experience been in these cases? Thanks again for your interest and rapid response, especially during the holiday season.

[Warren to Annie]

No problem! The $3500 would cover amending his asylum application as necessary, briefing the case and submitting supporting documents, and preparing for and conducting the trial on the asylum application. If we're unsuccessful and want to appeal, I'd have to charge additional fees. He has a pretty decent case, although he's still working on getting some more evidence that may or may not get here in time.

Asylum cases are the most difficult, but he definitely has a chance assuming the judge finds him credible, which I'm sure she will. I hope this helps!

[Annie to Warren]

I have found someone willing to underwrite a majority of the $3,500, making it possible to pay the fee. So please consider yourself hired, Warren. Let me know how/when we will pay you. Let me know if you need the money upfront before we leave for Thanksgiving celebrations in MN this Wednesday. And I'll hustle over to your office.

*****

TIMOTHY LEACOCK

November 16, 2016
God bless you, Ahmed,

    I hope this $20 helps.
    Enclosed, please find $20 for the account of Ahmed Mahamed Absame, MCC #24601-01.

Thank you,
Annie

    Although Ahmed was a trustee and could now hold a job in the kitchen, inmates were paid very little. He needed money to make phone calls to Zoya. And because long-distance calls to South Africa cost three dollars per minute, he could afford to converse only briefly a few times each week.

November 30, 2016
Dear Ahmed,

    I enjoyed yesterday's visit. I am also very hopeful for Tuesday's court hearing. I and an AIDVP friend plan to be there for your court hearing.

Peace,
Annie

7

Well-Founded Fear

> You wonder what his name is, where he came from… What
> lies or threats led him on this long march from home—
> if he would not rather have stayed there…in peace?
>
> —Fran Walsh, Philippa Boyens,
> Stephen Sinclair, and Peter Jackson,
> *Lord of the Rings: The Two Towers* (2002 film)

Michael

I met Ahmed vicariously through Annie, my spouse and fellow collaborator. I heard parts of Ahmed's story every week after Annie visited him in jail. The engineer in me was putting these accounts together in my mind. It seemed simple: Ahmed deserved asylum. If he were to be sent back to Somalia, Al-Shabaab would surely find and kill him. Even our ambassador, when he visited Somalia, never left the airport because he feared for his life. So when Annie said, "Ahmed needs the help of an immigration attorney. I want to find him one," I was totally on board.

Annie had looked in vain for free legal help. One organization showed promise and had an excellent track record but failed to get back to her after three weeks. When Warren Jackson spoke with the

AIDVP group, he made a favorable impression, especially on Annie. I was so glad that Annie, after checking with me, had hired him.

Because Warren was retained not long before Ahmed's hearing, he had to scramble to put together a prehearing brief. He filed the brief just in time. It contained every viable argument to support Ahmed's case for asylum. It was titled "Respondent's Updated Prehearing Brief and Statement in Support of Eligibility for Asylum, Withholding of Removal, and Relief under the Convention Against Torture [CAT]" (see "Appendix B: Types of Asylum"). The brief was thirty-seven pages, not counting a dozen pages of attachments. Copies were sent to the Immigration Court and the Office of Chief Legal Counsel for the Department of Homeland Security (DHS) by hand delivery.

I pored over the document, trying to understand the major arguments. I looked for whatever would give Ahmed a solid and clear case for asylum. I learned that back on July 11, 2016, the Chicago Asylum Office for US Citizenship and Immigration Services (DHS-USCIS-Chicago) had concluded that Ahmed had a credible fear of persecution on account of his political opinion if he were to be removed to Somalia. They based their determination on the interview notes made by US Customs and Border Protection (CBP) officials at the border.

Although this *credible fear of persecution* determination looked promising for Ahmed, it still had to be decided by an immigration judge. There were procedures to be followed.

The next step was to file a *Form I-589* (Application for Asylum and for Withholding of Removal) with the immigration court. He did this without help from legal counsel on September 7, 2016.

Because Ahmed did not possess a valid visa or entry document when he arrived at the border, USCIS had officially charged him with inadmissibility. His status became "In Removal Proceedings." That would change upon the judge's decision between one of two outcomes: either he could show, with the help of his attorney, his *eligibility for asylum* (the burden of proof was his), or he would be ordered to be *removed* back to Somalia.

An immigration judge would decide his case, but that was not the last word. Either Ahmed's attorney or the DHS counselor could appeal the decision to a higher court, the Board of Immigration Appeals (BIA). The BIA is a tribunal in Virginia that could either *remand* (send back) the case to the judge for further findings or order *removal* (deportation). The BIA was empowered to make their judgment in the case after reading the facts and arguments received from the immigration judge in her written decision and the appeal briefs submitted by both the DHS counselor and Ahmed's attorney.

Ahmed first had to show that he qualified as a *refugee* to be eligible for asylum. The law defined a refugee as any person who was unable or unwilling to return to the country of such person's nationality because of persecution or a well-founded fear of persecution on account of race, religion, nationality, membership in a particular social group, or political opinion. These were the so-called "five protected grounds."

Asylum status is a particular form of refugee status. For asylees, the applicant seeks protection at a port of entry or from within the borders of the United States. There were different laws and procedures for asylees and refugees. It was a little confusing, but once I understood these terms, I could narrow down the many rules that pertained to them, the legal procedures, and the consequences. I found out much about this way of proceeding on official Internet sites.

Attorney Jackson devoted much of his brief to the "protected grounds." Ahmed's political opinion, opposing that of Al-Shabaab and giving them a motive for persecution, comprised four factors:

First, Ahmed was threatened when he was at a state-run hospital applying for employment. Al-Shabaab targets Somali government officials and employees and anyone connected with the government.

Second, Ahmed is married to an Ethiopian. Her country invaded Somalia in 2006.

Third, Ahmed had fled Somalia during the diaspora in 1993, when large numbers of Somalis left the country during the civil war, and had returned to Somalia in 2016, which Al-Shabaab would perceive as not siding with their cause.

And fourth, Ahmed is a member of the Ashraf clan, which holds a privileged position with the Somali government.

Al-Shabaab could have targeted Ahmed for one or more of the preceding reasons, and all could be regarded as political motivation. Even if Ahmed did not hold these political opinions, as long as Al-Shabaab ascribed them to him, they could be considered "protected grounds."

The fact remained a terrorist organization had threatened Ahmed. In my way of thinking, it did not truly matter if Al-Shabaab had clear motives. It did not matter that they were acting rationally. You do not have time or inclination to ask about someone's motives when they are threatening to kill you.

Besides arguments for fear of persecution on one or more of the "protected grounds," Warren had to present in his brief to the judge that Ahmed's fear of persecution was both subjective and objective.

Subjective fear was based on Ahmed's testimony. But because Ahmed had very little tangible evidence to back up his testimony, his integrity and consistency in telling his story was crucial.

Objective fear, Warren argued, was based on country conditions, and he made three major points. First, the country reports were clear evidence of widespread violence in Somalia against individuals such as Ahmed. Second, if Ahmed had not left Somalia, he would have been defying direct orders from a terrorist organization that is well-known for carrying out their threats. Third, the Somali government has proved repeatedly to be ineffective in controlling Al-Shabaab or in protecting individuals such as Ahmed.

Warren added that Ahmed's fear objectively meets the standard of a ten percent chance of fear based on a protected ground. Simply put, Al-Shabaab insurgents, if defied, are effective in persecuting at least one in ten of the individuals they threaten. I kept marveling that the subtext of *persecution* meant *death* in Ahmed's case. "Face the consequences" was Al-Shabaab's euphemism.

Meanwhile, I researched online, investigating what I could find in similar cases and anything concerning the US government's responsibilities. It infuriated me that Ahmed was not in a detention facility like the one in Texas. But here he was, in Meadows County

Corrections, a weasel word for *jail*, a place to house offenders suspected or convicted of crimes. Yet Ahmed had committed no crime. He had asked for asylum and to stay alive!

Little by little, Annie enlightened me about Ahmed's treatment in jail. This contrasted significantly with detention policies:

> ICE is committed to ensuring that those in our custody reside in safe, secure, and humane environments and under *appropriate conditions of confinement* [emphasis mine]. ...
>
> In making such determinations, ERO [Enforcement and Removal Operations] officers weigh a variety of factors, including the person's criminal record, immigration history, ties to the community, risk of flight, and whether he or she poses a potential threat to public safety. (ICE 2022)

But in Ahmed's case, ERO-ICE, by handing him over to a correctional facility where he was treated like other inmates, largely gave up any oversight they might have had otherwise.

*****

On December 6, 2016, after Ahmed was detained for over five months in Meadows County Jail, an individual hearing was held in immigration court by Helen Alexander, an immigration judge, who had been appointed to that office by the US attorney general. At the hearing, two attorneys were present. On behalf of the government was Darcy Taylor, an assistant chief counsel for DHS-ICE, and on behalf of Ahmed (the respondent) was Warren Jackson, an immigration attorney.

During this hearing, DHS submitted two documents from South Africa that alleged Ahmed was a naturalized citizen of South Africa. Even though the evidence should have been submitted prior to the hearing, the judge admitted the two documents as exhibits 7 and 8. Exhibit 7 was a "Copy of Respondent's Purported Passport," while exhibit 8 was a "USCIS Letter" (outlining information obtained through inquiries with the South African Department of Home Affairs and the South African Police Service). Ahmed denied these had any validity. He stated that other than his picture, none of the other information was factual. Attorney Jackson argued this successfully, while Counselor Taylor could make no refutation.

Annie

I was at the hearing in quiet support of Ahmed, and I thought it went well. At the end of the hearing, the judge, Helen Alexander, announced that she was granting Ahmed asylum. Her written decision would be published about a week later.

I was elated! As I was leaving the courtroom, I talked briefly with Warren. His reaction to the proceedings was good, but he cautioned me that the attorney for DHS would probably appeal. "How long does it usually take for a judge to write up a decision?" I asked.

"I'd expect to have it by early or midweek," he said. "But keep in mind that she's a brand-new judge. It might take longer than usual. Judges don't like to be overturned on appeal, so she might try to make the decision as airtight as possible, which would also explain any delay."

December 9, 2016
Dear Ahmed,

>If all goes well, you will not receive this letter because the Judge has written up her decision, and your attorney has gotten you out of jail and into the Iowa community. But things often get delayed, so I am sending this just in case, so you will know what is going on.
>
>As I will be out of town for the holidays, a wonderful family I have known for years will

come to get you after you are released and welcome you into their home. They have three children. The father is a high school teacher, and the mother works in social justice. They are very excited about your coming to stay with them. Other people from our community also want to help. I expect you will meet a number of them also.

We are so blessed with the judge's favorable decision! I know the prosecution will appeal in about 30 days. As they say in America, "We're not out of the woods yet." But we'll take that as it comes. Your attorney knows what he's doing.

I was going to send a book on writing resumes (CVs), but we'll send for that after you are released.

Peace,
Annie

*****

It surprised me to get a letter from Ahmed. All he had was my name. He went through the trouble of asking someone in the jail to find my address from their visitor's records and then address it to me.

Dec 12, 2016
Dear Annie,

I hope that you are well. Every time I talk to you is special. I enjoy every moment of it. I am thankful for everything you have done for me.

I want to thank you for coming to my court hearing. It meant a lot to me; no one was there for me except Warren and you. Your presence in the court has given me much-needed courage—I felt calm and happy. It was a big day, and you were there for me.

Mr. Warren represented me very well. He has given his best shot. He had spent a lot of time on my case, his efforts were clear, and I was happy with the outcome. I will see what happens next.

My court hearing was supposed to be at 1 o'clock. Instead, it started at 3. I was sorry to keep you waiting that long. You had other commitments, but because of the delay, you could not complete your day's tasks.

I have received your letter and cards, which you sent on November 30th. All of the cards were special—the card with the quote from Mahatma Gandhi was outstanding.

Give my regards to Michael and your family. I will be looking forward to seeing you in January. Stay in peace and good health.

Regards,
Ahmed

Michael

On December 13, 2016, the immigration judge published her decision. After including long paragraphs on background, procedural history, documentary evidence presented by Warren Jackson, testimonial evidence by Ahmed, and the country conditions of Somalia, she outlined her findings on Ahmed's credibility.

Judge Alexander found Ahmed responded well to the questions asked by her, Counselor Taylor, and Attorney Jackson. She said Ahmed was believable, internally consistent, and consistent with all evidence presented, in particular the Department of State reports on Somalia and Al-Shabaab.

Credibility was crucial. Without that going for him, Ahmed's case would be over. But many other factors played into the judge's decision. After defining *asylum* in her written decision, Judge Alexander laid out her findings and analysis, supported by a great deal of precedent, which I have summarized:

- *Level of harm.* The court found that the harm Ahmed suffered was severe enough to be past persecution. Ahmed's credible testimony concerning the two death threats he received from Al-Shabaab gave evidence of this.
- *Protected ground.* The court found that the past harm that Ahmed suffered and the likely future persecution at the hands of Al-Shabaab are based on (1) his imputed political opinion, (2) having an Ethiopian spouse, and (3) being a member of the Ashraf clan.
- *Country conditions.* Because the Somalia government is unwilling or unable to control Al-Shabaab, Ahmed has shown a well-founded fear of persecution in Somalia based on the death threats he received.

The court document ended with Judge Alexander's order granting Ahmed asylum, and she authorized it with her signature.

But there was a huge problem, as you shall see. Other than a note that exhibits 7 and 8 were entered as evidence, the judge wrote nothing about them, their refutation. Nevertheless, the DHS counselor used them in her appeal. This was a tactic that clearly took advantage of an oversight by the judge. And because the board relies only on what is written and mailed to them, they did not know that these two exhibits were successfully discredited by the judge.

But at this point, we directed our thoughts to hoping that ICE would release Ahmed from jail. After all, the judge had ruled for asylum! We expected an appeal by DHS, but ICE now had no reason to continue to keep him locked up. He could stay with the O'Malley's over the holidays and then with Annie and me once we got back from California.

8

On the Threshold

A doorway is a passage, not a place of residence.

—Craig D. Lounsbrough

Annie

December 15, 2016
Hello Ahmed,

    I hope you are not receiving this letter and that your release has already happened! But just in case, know we are all thinking of you and praying for the best for you and all your family.
    Soon you will be out and about in Arabella, learning more about the American culture and better able to communicate with your own beloved family.

Peace, my friend,
Annie

    After I was so confident in my letter with Ahmed, I thought I'd better check in with Warren.

Emails: December 16, 2016
Subject: Jail release and name spelling

[Annie to Warren]

Hello Warren, I hope you are getting some rest in the days up to Christmas. I wonder if you noticed, but the cover page of the judge's decision document has Ahmed's name spelled wrong. Will that cause a problem?

[Warren to Annie]

Thanks, Annie. I noticed the typo too. No worries. In the immigration world, all you are is a number—an "alien registration number," that is.

[Annie to Warren]

That's good. And my big question: now that we have the judge's decision, are we waiting for anything else before Kate and Martin get Ahmed out of jail?

[Warren to Annie]

We are just waiting on ICE to give their okay. As I stated before, they are fighting it, but I think I found an internal memo that should settle the issue and result in his release. But it's totally their call. I'll follow up with ICE again today and let you know.

It was over a week later. I was waiting and waiting, and I was getting antsy, so I sent an email to Warren for an update.

TIMOTHY LEACOCK

Emails: December 27–28, 2016
Subject: Follow up on Ahmed

[Annie to Warren]

Hello Warren! I hope you had a relaxing, renewing holiday.

It's been two weeks since the Judge's favorable decision came down for Ahmed. I know we are awaiting the Government's response to see if they will contest it. I also know you've sent in more info to strengthen the Judge's decision. So…is it a good or bad sign that we have heard nothing from them? Could they

- not be moving because of the holiday, or
- not be moving because they are building up a case, or
- not be moving because they have decided not to fight and are just letting the 30-day period for contesting run out?

It's all a big question mark for us. But, then again, perhaps you've seen patterns over the years. Any ideas?

[Warren to Annie]

Unfortunately, I received confirmation today that DHS is appealing. The notice of appeal has been filed. They have listed what I would consider bogus grounds along with at least one valid ground (*firm resettlement* in South Africa). But there are grounds for attacking this either in my appeal brief, or if there is a remand to the Immigration Judge on this issue.

[Annie to Warren]

Does that mean Ahmed stays in jail some more?

[Warren to Annie]

Yes. They are keeping him detained while the appeal is pending. I have tried to convince them otherwise. And what is maddening is that they haven't given me any reasons for holding him.

[Annie to Warren]

You have tried your best, Warren.

[Warren to Annie]

Once the resettlement issue is settled, I will try again. To continue with the case, I will have to charge more for the response to the appeal. I will charge another $2000, plus postage. If the case is remanded—a real possibility—I would have to charge more for a subsequent trial. Do you have any questions for me?

[Annie to Warren]

Very well, and thank you for the update.

I do have some questions. But I need a little time to pull them together. I got a call today with bad news about my disabled daughter. And then a few minutes later I got a call saying my mom is going into hospice care. So I'm sad and tired.

[Warren to Annie]

So sorry to hear that.

[Annie to Warren]

We're flying back to Arabella early tomorrow. I'll get back to you soon after that with our questions. Thanks for your attentive care around this case.

*****

Michael and I sat with our son Charlie and his wife, Marie. We were visiting them and our two grandkids in California. Charlie and Marie were our moral and financial support as we sought how we could best help Ahmed. They both had hearts that reached out to people in need and had been firmly supportive during our work in Africa.

After talking it over, we all agreed we would keep moving forward with fighting Ahmed's case, but it would mostly depend on Ahmed. *Could he take the strain?*

Once we arrived back home, I contacted Warren. "We are willing to hire you to respond to the appeal," I said. "We all hope the appeal's court will uphold the immigrant judge's ruling, and that will be the end of it. As promised, here are some questions we have. Number 1: if the case is remanded, will it be around the issue of South African citizenship? And if that is the case, wouldn't we need additional evidence to be successful in that new trial?"

"Yes, if the case is remanded, it will likely be on the issue of his citizenship," Warren said, "and both parties can present evidence on this issue. The worst-case scenario is that the judge says he's a South African. If that happens, we file for asylum from South Africa. He was shot and assaulted there numerous times for being an immigrant.

"But we still have a strong argument against South African citizenship. His children's birth certificates from South Africa will prove that at least two of them were born there before the US government claims his wife arrived in South Africa! So if the case is remanded, I'll submit the birth certificates. I should get them soon."

"Taking this a step further," I asked, "if the judge again rules in our favor in the new trial, can the prosecution appeal again?"

"Yes, if we win the case after remand, regardless of whether it's asylum from Somalia or South Africa, DHS could still appeal. And obviously, we would appeal if we lost the case.

"Now, as far as custody, if we win on appeal, he'll be released."

"And if the case is remanded, does he stay in jail?"

"If that happens, I could file a motion for a bond hearing, but I'll only do this if Ahmed wishes. He has always been eligible for bond but not right now while the DHS appeal is pending. Only the immigration judge can issue a bond, and I can ask for one the next time there is a hearing. I explained all this to Ahmed over the phone today."

"I am wondering about the timeline for these scenarios," I said. "Ahmed's family is barely hanging on, and we have all seen cases where asylum applicants are stuck in jail for extended periods. We need to know how Ahmed and his family feel about all this."

"It doesn't look like Ahmed wants to be out on bond. He knows that if that should happen, the process slows down," Warren said. "And as far as timeline, our response to the DHS appeal will probably be due in the next month or two. Then the timeline becomes uncertain."

December 30, 2016
Dear Annie,

I hope you and your family are well—I am doing fine. I have received all the letters and beautiful cards which you sent me. There are no words that can explain my gratitude.

Mr. Warren has tried his best to get me out of jail. ICE would not allow that until my case is finalized. Good things come to those who wait—my time will come. Late is better than never.

Martin came to visit me. It was nice talking to him; he is a kind and gentle man. I look forward to staying with him and his family once I am released.

As expected, the prosecutor has filed an appeal. That process will take from three to six months. God knows best. I have every reason to be grateful and happy since you came into my life—my spirit is high; I am full of hope and happiness.

As 2016 comes to an end, I want to wish you and your family everything of the best.

Thank you, Annie.

Regards,
Ahmed

Our plan for Ahmed to stay with the O'Malleys over the holidays fell through. Because of the DHS appeal, we would hear nothing about a release until a decision from the BIA, which could take months.

Email: January 1, 2017
Subject: A bit of info

[Kate to Annie]

Hi Annie. Happy New Year!

We are so sad that we never got to host Ahmed. Martin was able to visit him, and we hope to do so again—either in or out of confinement.

We have the clothes you gave us, plus a jacket, some pajamas, and a shirt that we got for him. I leave for the Dominican Republic on

Tuesday, but Martin is not teaching this week and may be able to bring them to your house.

Prayers continue for him and his family.

*****

January 15, 2017
Hello Ahmed!

    I am so sorry I could not visit this week. A sheet of ice covered the driveway; people were falling on the sidewalks and smacking into each other with their cars. So I figured it was best to stay home.
    I read your three letters with a mug of tea. Thank you so much for taking the time to write and using your precious resources on stamps. Your sentiments were well expressed and much appreciated.
    Your patience and courage in these difficult circumstances are extraordinary.
    Greet Zoya for me when you next talk on the phone.
    You and your family remain in our prayers.

                                              Annie

Emails: January 28, 2017
Subject: Somali Refugee Ban

[Annie to Warren and Marie]

    What effect does Trump's order barring Somalis have on Ahmed's case? Could it keep him from staying in the USA even if the Virginia court also upholds Asylum? Could it keep the Virginia Court from remanding his case?

Dang. I am so ashamed of our President. He can't handle a dismissive tweet but shuts the door on those suffering real bombs, bullets, murder, and torture. I am really TO'd today.

[Warren to Annie and Marie]

It shouldn't affect him because he's already here and applying for asylum, but since they are singling out Somalis from coming here in the first place right now, there might be some residual effect. They were already fighting this case pretty hard, and it will probably only increase under this new Administration.

I'm more worried about getting his wife and kids here if we still succeed in Ahmed's case. They are not letting in any Somalis for at least 120 days, but I can see this being much longer unless the courts continue to push back. Excellent victory tonight on the national stay for those being detained at airports. Stay tuned.

I got an explosive email response from my daughter-in-law, who is active politically, sending postcards encouraging people to vote. She was referring to my emails with Warren:

Email: January 29, 2017
Subject: Somali Refugee Ban

[Marie to Annie]

This is so disappointing! Ugh. There are no words for this kind of human treatment. It pisses me off that this comes from a party of "so-called" conservative Christians. Jesus would never behave this way.

February 16, 2017
Hello Ahmed!

    Thanks for the meeting on Wednesday. I'm so glad you could make it down.

    I look forward to hearing about what you have learned in the whopping 900+ page GED (General Educational Development) study book. Talk about a challenge! It will be a refresher for me as well.

    I will continue to make new cards and was wondering about a couple of things. Are there any particular images of Muslim faith and worship that would be a comfort to receive? Also, are any specific texts that might do the same? Are texts from the Christian Bible helpful? As you said, you're not a good Muslim if you don't know about Jesus. Anyway, I seek your advice.

                           Have a blessed day,
                                    Annie

March 1, 2017
Hello again, Ahmed!

    I am so glad that you have been accepted into the GED classes, that you are excused from work while you are studying, and that any exam you take in jail will be good at the Community College when you get out. Also, having a skilled personal teacher is an asset for moving forward and will be another connection in the Arabella community.

You, your case, and your family remain in my thoughts and prayers—greetings to Zoya. In a few months, God willing, you will be able to make a cup of hot tea and talk with her for as long as you wish on Skype when you get out.

We all remain in God's grace and time.

Annie

*****

Three months passed since Ahmed was granted asylum, and he was still in jail. Everyone was waiting for the board's ruling. Would the BIA uphold Judge Alexander's decision, or would they *remand* it for more proceedings?

Emails: March 13, 2017
Subject: Ahmed

[Warren to Annie]

Here's a copy of my appeal brief that I submitted to the Board of Immigration Appeals on Friday. My brief and the Government brief are due simultaneously on 3/14 after the Government asked for and received a three-week extension. I guess we could still have a decision by the end of April.

[Annie to Warren]

WOW. This is an impressive document. It's a thorough, detailed, and solid defense for Ahmed. A lot of work went into the document. And a lot of experience and care. I continue to pray for you and all involved in the upcoming hearing. And I'm hopeful Ahmed will be released.

For all that you have done for Ahmed, THANK YOU. And thank you for all you do for so many others, which matters so incredibly much.

Email: March 13, 2017
Subject: Ahmed update

[Annie to Charlie and Marie]

I'll see Ahmed tomorrow. He remains in high spirits, studying hard for a GED in a class that detainees usually cannot join. But the teacher heard he was studying alone and invited him to class every day for 1.5 hours each morning. He works in the kitchen for about seven hours a day at 40 cents an hour. Exercises and prays. That fills his days.

March 24, 2017
Hello Ahmed!

Sorry I was not able to visit this week. Jury duty took a lot of time and energy. But it was important to do. I expect to make the next visit with no problems.
I hope you received the book, *Awaken Your Strongest Self*, Amazon said it was delivered on Tuesday.
My daughter-in-law is signing up this week at the Meadows County jail site, so she'll be able to meet you during their April visit to Arabella.

I know you will enjoy her. She is tiny but has so much energy, especially for justice issues.

I suspect you will not receive this until after our visit, but I figure it's always nice to write it out. And also, if something comes up where I can't get to the jail, you know all the news that I have!

I look forward to seeing your GED papers, the progress you are making, and learning more about the jail's educational programs.

We are all well and waiting for Spring to warm up the ground, flowers, and birdies.

Peace,
Annie

April 4, 2017
Dear Ahmed,

An enjoyable visit today.

I've got to cut back and send only two cards soon. My supply is going down! Subconsciously, I guess I'm counting on your release in a few months.

Next week is Holy Week for us Christians. You will likely be entering into Ramadan as the results of the [BIA decision] grow closer.

Keep up the routine that is building strong social, emotional, spiritual, intellectual, and physical muscles. You are using this time very, very wisely.

Blessings,
Annie

Emails: April 25, 2017
Subject: Updates on Ahmed?

[Annie to Warren]

When I call the number for information on Mahamed-Absame, Ahmed's case, it no longer says the appeal (by the Government) is pending, but instead that there is no information about an appeal. Nor is there any information about when case paperwork was filed like there used to be.

Does this mean that the information is not available because they are updating the system, or might there have been a decision in Virginia about the case?

I'm sorry to bother you if the change is due to their upgrading info. Ahmed and I (I just saw him) would like to know what you think. He hasn't been able to sleep, feeling a decision might have come down.

[Warren to Annie]

I checked my account online, and a decision was issued on 4/21. I won't know the outcome until I receive it in the mail. However, my best guess is that it was remanded back to the judge for further proceedings as anticipated.

I can't remember if I told you this, but upon receiving his complete file, I noticed that he was designated as an "arriving alien" when he came to the US, which prevents a judge from granting a bond. I could try to fight this, but it will be difficult and maybe impossible since Ahmed previously admitted it before he had counsel. Technically, everyone caught at the border is an arriving alien, but many are released by ICE on parole. Unfortunately, that is not Ahmed, so he might have to wait this out behind bars. Thanks, and I will update you as I receive more information.

[Annie to Warren]

Thank you for the rapid reply, Warren.

I anticipated his case was relatively strong, and the local judge's decision to be supported in Virginia.

I had been wondering why Ahmed could not get out on bail. I believe Ahmed told me he was offered bail initially, but refused it because he had no funds. So why couldn't he get it when funds were available later? You'd have to double-check with him about this.

Honestly, I don't know if his family could take the waiting for another six months or a year. They are strained almost beyond strength right now—barely hanging on—let alone waiting out another stretch of Ahmed in jail. He might opt to give up. With him out on bond, it would be a lot easier.

9

Don't You Have Some Place Else to Live?

> Law in origin was merely a codification of the power of dominant groups, and did not aim at anything that to a modern man would appear to be justice.
>
> —Bertrand Russell

Michael

Ahmed's attorney told us that an appeal by DHS was unusual in asylum cases. Usually, it was the respondent who would appeal after an unfavorable ruling by the judge. In addition, although an appeal by DHS was pending, it was customary for ICE to release the respondent from detention. But when Warren asked the deputy chief counselor, who was in charge of such matters, he had refused to release Ahmed. Was there a reason? He gave none.

The gist of the DHS appeal document was that the immigration judge *erred* because

- the judge failed to address the issue of firm resettlement based on evidence Ahmed lived in South Africa for the past nineteen years,
- the evidence failed to show that Ahmed's harm rose to the level of past persecution in Somalia during his five-day visit,
- the evidence failed to show that Ahmed established a well-founded fear of future persecution, and
- the judge found Ahmed's testimony credible.

Basically, every basis that the immigration judge used to support her decision for asylum was called into question. To me, this was the proverbial "throw everything at the wall and see what sticks." *How could the judge err on all counts?*

In Attorney Jackson's document, "Respondent's Brief in Opposition to DHS Appeal," four pages were devoted to facts, procedural history, and standard of review. Then the argument section followed with all the ways the judge ruled correctly. This consumed nine full pages, was clearly laid out, and addressed what DHS claimed were errors in the judge's ruling.

And Warren added that DHS's sudden claim Ahmed was a citizen of South Africa, besides being false, did not follow proper procedure. Concerning DHS's exhibits 7 and 8, Warren found that they were untimely submitted, it was improper for the judge to admit them into evidence, and the judge did not give him the opportunity to object. And because Ahmed's attorney could not cross-examine the author of exhibit 8, it violated Ahmed's due process rights.

Warren grudgingly seemed to accept the above procedural violations, but he did not want the BIA to be distracted by this. Instead, he asserted the real crux of the matter: that the judge had analyzed both exhibits and found that the alleged facts contained in them were not credible.

In the conclusion of his brief, Warren requested the BIA to agree with the immigration judge and thus grant Ahmed asylum.

Annie

April 26, 2017
Hello Ahmed,

It's cold and wet outside today. Ugh. I could use a little sunshine today to splash around inside and out.

I checked with your lawyer, Ahmed, and apparently, there *has* been a decision [by the BIA] in your case. But he does not know what it is and will not know until he gets written confirmation in the mail. He will let you know when he hears anything.

I remain very hopeful. However, it will be essential for you (maybe with Zoya) to sit and pray about all the possible outcomes. As hard as it is, there is the possibility of your case getting remanded. I'm not sure what all that means in terms of time, but it would be good to ask yourself, "what would it take for me and my family to hang on through more court hearings?" In all honesty, would that be a non-starter? A possibility? The boogie man in the room wants to stay in the shadows.

Ahmed, I inadvertently screwed up and broke a jail rule. I just wasn't thinking. I set it up for Marie [my daughter-in-law] to interview you while she was in town. She's very interested in refugee/immigrant issues, primarily as they affect Africans.

Here's the deal. I forgot that as a relative of an AIDVP volunteer (me), she should not have come into the jail to visit you. It set off bells in the Jail staff. I learned yesterday that I could not continue to see you until they get a satisfactory explanation for the violation. The AIDVP coordinator and I spoke yesterday. I explained my dumb mistake and asked for mercy. She is carrying my words to the Programs Coordinator. I don't know what they will decide. They could say, "You screwed up, lady. Don't do it again," and put the fear of God in me, which is already there, and let me continue to see you. There is, however, the possibility that the jail might bar me from coming to see you anymore because of the violation. I have no control over their decision.

I feel foolish and embarrassed about this. Worst of all, I feel seriously bummed that it adds a level of pain and uncertainty to you when you already carry so much. Please forgive me.

As I am ever coaxing boogie men out of the closet (they dance in the sunlight), I look to possible outcomes. They could send in a different AIDVP volunteer if I get the boot. Or perhaps Martin could come and visit more often. He's a great guy. Rest assured that my prayers and concern for you and your family will remain here.

Blessings and deep peace,
Annie

Michael

On April 21, 2017, after reviewing the judge's written decision and the briefs by DHS and respondent, the BIA ordered a remand, a return of the case to the immigration court.

The BIA was looking for more fact-finding and analysis concerning the firm resettlement issue. In this remand, they were giving the immigration judge an opportunity, based on this issue, to reassess her decision about Ahmed's eligibility for asylum. If it could be established that Ahmed and his family had found another country with a path to citizenship, someplace else to live, then he would not be considered for asylum in the US but sent back to South Africa.

The BIA was correct in asking for more information. They could not rely simply on Attorney Jackson's arguments. They had to see it in the judge's written decision.

Still, I thought it was misleading for the DHS to include this in their appeal. It was easy to see by even a nonlawyerly person like me that the *evidence* had multiple errors in what it claimed to be true. For example, how could Ahmed be issued a South African identity number at the time of his supposed naturalization in 2010 but then be issued another identity number in 2016 related to his temporary refugee status? All the immigration judge had to do was write this refutation into her decision. Then there wouldn't be any need for a BIA remand to discover this information in a new hearing.

The questionable tactics of the DHS counselor and the mistake of the judge produced a delay that easily could have been avoided. Meanwhile, Ahmed sat in jail, waiting and worrying. *But at least the board did not rule unfavorably.*

I was convinced it was almost over. The BIA had based their remand on the firm resettlement issue. Warren would spell it out clearly for the judge, who could put it all in writing in her next ruling, and then DHS would have no basis to appeal again. I stayed with that thought while we all waited because it was reasonable, offered some measure of comfort, and gave me hope.

10

Justice Will Prevail

No matter who you are, no matter where
you come from, you are beautiful.

—Michelle Obama

Annie

Emails: April 27, 2017
Subject: About the Ahmed Case

[Annie to Warren]

The sun is out today, and the crabby factor is going down. I might even plant some flowers.

Could someone from your staff take the wire transfer information over to Ahmed if I deliver the info to your office? I can't leave any papers with him when I visit. It's too much info for him to memorize very accurately. And I am not comfortable sending the information through the PO jail mail. Thanks for considering.

[Warren to Annie]

Absolutely. I plan on visiting him next week. I also received the decision today. I have attached it. We're now just awaiting another court date. Unfortunately, I will have to re-bill since we'll have to do yet another trial, plus at least one or two preliminary hearings. I'm happy to discuss more, if necessary, too.

[Annie to Warren]

Before we go to court again, we need to know Ahmed's wishes because his family is barely hanging on. They will all be hugely disappointed at this news. Also, we need to know about the chances of winning the case. I thought we gave this trial the best we had, but we are back to the beginning (I think) again. Are we starting all over? The donors need to know there is a fundamental difference this time around.

If the chances are not a lot better than before, and Ahmed is not assertive about fighting his case, the donors might give Ahmed funds and get him back to his family. Another trial and possible remand could mean over six months more in jail since he can't get out. His wife and three kids have no financial support while he is gone. And communication with her [by Ahmed] from behind bars is a struggle—a big-time bummer.

Alas, I am sure these kinds of stories are not new to you.

Unfortunately, due to a glitch—I inadvertently broke a jail rule—I am barred from seeing Ahmed myself until we get the thing straightened out. So, for now, if Ahmed wants the donors to know anything about his wishes, it will have to come through you—or snail mail to me.

[Warren to Annie]

I spoke to Ahmed. He knows. DHS gave him a copy of the decision as well. I explained things to him, including all scenarios. I'm also going to call DHS tomorrow to discuss his release. I'm not sure they'll budge, but I have to try. It's asinine. He's not a flight risk or danger to the community, but I think they'll come back with the identity issue.

The judge is on our side, and I think it will stay that way. It's easy to say, I know, but I think I can make this work. The worst-case scenario is that the judge says he's a South African citizen, and we apply for asylum from there. (He was shot there as part of a xenophobic attack.) Not a bad backup plan. I understand his family is suffering—as is Ahmed—but if we can win this, he can help his family come here, assuming the courts keep blocking Trump's travel/Muslim ban. We'll probably just have two more hearings, including a mini-trial on firm resettlement. I'll continue to charge a discounted rate. This time another $2500. I'll talk to Ahmed and let you know what he says, but I'll try to expedite this so that we can hopefully get another decision from the judge in the next 60 days.

[Annie to Warren]

Thank you for all your work on this, Warren. Every bit of it and your thoughtful approach is appreciated.

Michael and I need to meet with you for a short while. We're trying to understand the scenarios and only seem to raise more questions. Two heads are not always better than one.

After the remand by BIA, it seemed like Ahmed's fight for asylum in the courts was starting anew. And he had been in the US for almost a year now. Yet he was determined—with his lawyer—to enter this next round of the match. And Michael and I were firmly in support. If he was up for this battle, so were we.

*****

Although I was still banned from visiting Ahmed, I needed to get some information to him directly, not through the mail. I wanted to send some funds to Zoya and have Ahmed explain the details about receiving them to her by phone, so I emailed the Western Union info to Warren, who agreed to hand deliver it to Ahmed at the jail.

May 2, 2017
Hello there, Ahmed,

I hope you stay true to your self-care course at this very unsettling time. All the habits you've learned are essential for keeping an even keel for yourself and your family. By the way, I started reading "Awaken Your Strongest Self" but am only a few pages into it. It will make good discussion material when I visit again.

The AIDVP Coordinator hopes to check with the Programs Manager tomorrow (Wednesday) to see if all is smoothed out regarding my mistake, and I can resume visits. Sometimes there are delays in the two of them getting together, however. I hope to know more in 24 hours. But honestly, the way the world is going these days, one wonders if the sun will start coming up a day late, tardy like most humans on the planet and every department of the government. *Patience, Annie. Patience.*

I spoke with Warren this morning, who gave me further details on where your legal matters stand. This will be very helpful as I listen to you, your situation, and your desires for the next step. I suspect you will need to talk more to Zoya these days, as efforts on her part could be key in helping address the Government's challenges to your case. Martin intends to ensure you have the funds to stay connected with her. I know those international calls suck in the money. I believe he wants to visit you on Friday.

I understand all the positive elements Warren has about the remand of your case and how he plans to address the conflicting data on citizenship. He is pretty confident he can provide what is needed in a mini-trial and win it. There are no guarantees, though. From my perspective, it is vital to remember that the more documentation Zoya can provide for your case, the higher the level of certainty for a win and the lower the chances that the mini-trial would once again result in a government challenge which would send the case back to Virginia [BIA] again.

Ultimately, you have to decide how much and how long I should fight. What are the risks of winning and losing? What are the long- and short-term advantages of the legal approach? A scenario you might consider (if the case doesn't carry the kind of certainty you hoped for) is ending the legal fight and going home. At which point, independent donor and community resources earmarked for court or early resettlement of your family might be reassigned as direct family aid for reestablishing back in South Africa.

Lots to think about…

You and your family remain in my prayers and thoughts. Hopefully, I will see you again on Tuesday, May 9. If I (and the rising sun) *do* get hung up, I will write a letter with the latest developments.

Blessings and peace,
Annie

May 6, 2017
Dear Annie,

I hope that you are well. I am fine. Zoya and the kids are fine too. I received the outcome of [the appeal] on April 26th—it has been remanded.

I came to America looking for protection for myself and my family. Justice will prevail. I am ready to sacrifice my freedom, health, and myself as a whole—I will remain in jail if that will guarantee me asylum status. This, too, shall pass. I have nowhere to return.

The package [of books] came at the right time and was vital for Zoya and the kids. It's the beginning of winter in South Africa. It's also the second term for the kids. Toward the end of May, it will be Ramadan fasting month. You came to my rescue once again.

I am relieved and happy that you will be allowed to visit me. When I received your letter, I was down and sad—your visit means so much to me. You have helped me a lot…if they didn't let you visit me, that would have been the end of me. Thank God that you will continue to visit.

Please give my regards to Michael. May God bless you and your family.

Regards,
Ahmed

11

Day after Day

> When things were very bad, his soul just crawled behind his heart and curled up and went to sleep.
>
> —Maya Angelou, *I Know Why the Caged Bird Sings*

Ahmed

It was a Monday morning after breakfast, and inmates were heading back to their beds. "Please wake me up if my name is being called out," said one of the inmates to me.

"I will wake you. I promise," I said.

The time was twelve noon. The officer on duty said on a high-volume speaker, "If I call your name, you have some mail. Please come and collect it." Then I heard, "Bed 14," so I rushed to collect my letter.

Only two or three guys' names were called out, and everyone looked at the letter recipients. The atmosphere in the room changed, and many inmates spoke their minds. Emotions were running high. "I was not a bad person. I thought my family loved me, but that is not the case," one inmate said. "No one remembers me or sends me a letter or card. I am really sad."

"I used to share everything with my family and friends, and now they have turned their back on me," another one said. "Mahamed, you are very lucky. You receive letters and cards every week. Your family loves you."

The time was 12:45 p.m. All the inmates were getting ready for work. And I contemplated whether I should open the letter and see the cards now or open it tonight. I made a last-minute decision: I will open the letter tonight when I have more time. So I put it under my pillow, and I went to work with a huge grin on my face.

My shift was seven hours in the kitchen, preparing the food for the evening meal and doing whatever tasks the cook asked me to do. As I was putting away things from the noon meal, a guard approached me and asked for some food. But I refused. It was against jail rules. "Strip-search," he commanded, with a look in his eyes that said, "I'm in charge here," and a grin that told me what he was thinking: *This oughta be fun.*

I knew not to say anything but to comply quietly. This was not my first time, nor would it be my last. With my jail clothes dropped and lying around my ankles, I felt embarrassed while he searched me but with no shame. To keep my dignity, I said a prayer for him.

Others who worked in the kitchen suffered the same at the end of their shifts. The guards were looking for weapons and contraband. The only weapons in sight were potato and carrot peelers, and these were all accounted for. Any other cutting tools were locked up, just like I was when I returned to my cell.

It was 7:45 p.m. All the inmates were heading back to unit 3. "I hate this place," said one inmate.

The responses were understandable from everyone else. No one wanted to be here, including me. A long night awaited everyone's loneliness and regrets, and sometimes, tears were common among the men.

It was 11:45 p.m. By now, I had taken a shower, dealt with my GED homework, and practiced my Spanish with some guys in my mod. I sipped my thin coffee and opened my letter with joy. I saw three cards carrying messages of hope, encouragement, and love. Suddenly, everything made sense, and a clear message emerged:

> Never give up, Ahmed; we are there for you; you are not alone, and the end of your journey is getting closer.

This was the best encouragement someone in jail could get.

It was twelve midnight, and the lights of nearby buildings were turned off. Another clock I could not touch but could see from my bed through a tiny window high in the wall. As I prepared for bed, I was feeling happy and hopeful. I touched my head to the floor in prayer. God had indeed blessed me on this day.

As I lay in my bunk, my thoughts went to my special friend. *Annie, the word thank you is not good enough. Thank you from the bottom of my heart. You have made a huge contribution to my life. I will ever be grateful to God for all the bounties and blessings of your visits that have been bestowed on me.*

Tomorrow, many will ask me to share the cards I received. The artwork was always beautiful, and the famous quotes were inspiring. I could count on one or other of the inmates to say, "What is the word for today, Mahamed?" And then I would share the cards all around.

12

Bare Necessities

It is the heart that makes a man rich. He is rich according to what he is, not according to what he has.

—Henry David Beecher (1813)

Annie

Ahmed said that you were always hungry if you didn't have at least some money in your account. You wouldn't have any money to buy food to supplement what you were given at mealtime, which he described as pretty unappetizing. The food they bought for the inmates was in large bulk quantities, and it was always about ready to expire. These rations did not appeal to many people, and there often wasn't enough to eat, especially for the larger individuals, so they would go to the commissary or the vending machines (not sure if those terms are interchangeable). There, they would get honey buns and instant coffee in packets. Later in the evening, they would get the warmest water from the bathroom faucet to make the instant coffee and then sit and have it with their honey buns, and that was like the highlight of the evening, just to have those extra treats.

Martin put some money in Ahmed's jail account more than once, which absolutely made Ahmed's day. He gained weight after a while even though he exercised a lot in his cell. The fatty food and the lack of consistency in being out and about made him put some weight around his middle.

Sometimes, inmates would take a honey bun, a glazed one that consisted of flour and a lot of sugar; mix it with water; and put it in a container. They would hide it under their beds so it would ferment and make a kind of juice, something that would make them high. They would drink the solution, become intoxicated, and spend some time away from the realities of jail.

Ramen noodles were a constant in the jail, and I think they charged like two dollars a package, which sold for twenty-five cents outside the jail. The high costs were a hardship because they worked for something like three dollars a day.

Frequently, when an inmate would be released, he would give the contents of his locker to the people he liked in the jail. Either he passed on the key or just emptied his locker. Most often, it was extra food, which was treated like money in the inmate barter system. It wasn't worth much outside, so it was easy to give to others, perhaps someone who had befriended him in jail.

Ahmed absolutely loved working in the kitchen. The cook there was a fantastic guy who would give the workers some extra food. He treated them with compassion and respect. Several of them spoke Spanish, and Ahmed loved learning Spanish from this cook, so the kitchen was a place to have a friend. They could talk together in Spanish as they labored. The cook appreciated Ahmed for his work. He did a great job, and it was a break from being out with the other men in his *mod*.

Ahmed fasted for Ramadan, and some guards were very good, bringing his food at four o'clock before sunrise and being respectful and quiet. Others were awful. They would make sure that everybody woke up when they brought the food, or they would call him when it was too late, and the food came and went, or they didn't care to call him at all. So it depended upon the whims of the guards how much Ahmed would be hungry.

I wanted to send him a prayer rug and other things directly from Amazon. But at Amazon, all the prayer rugs had a sewn-in compass, and compasses were not allowed. Later on, mailing packages became worse. Drugs were starting to arrive in delivered parcels, so they would not let things come in—surprisingly from Amazon as well—because they said some inmates had contacts who could fake even that kind of delivery.

Having a job as a trustee, wearing the clothes of a trustee, was a huge deal. You got more respect from the guards. That meant you could do some jobs that were available in the jail, giving you a certain amount of money, a bit of extra cash for food or maybe for the phone calls. You couldn't make very much as a trustee, but it got you out of the *mod* and out and about with people, talking to other folks like the cook. And having a little money in your pocket felt good.

International phone calls were stressful because they were a dollar a minute. And what do you say to your loved ones when you can talk to them for one, two, or three minutes, and as you're talking, there goes the whole money you made for that day? The family does not quite understand what's going on with you, and you have so much you want to say. You want to tell them about what's happened to you and what you hope will be the best for them. Much of a phone call would be saying, "Hello, how are you?" and "I love you," back and forth. How much time would that leave for all that is left to be said?

As far as I know, Ahmed never went outside. There was a time each day when they could go out to exercise, but he did not want to go out. Too many of the men out there would get into fights, and if you got into fights, you could get hurt. You could lose your privileges. You could get on somebody's wrong side, and they would be after you. He used to stare through a small window high in the wall outside his cell. One time he asked me, "What is that building, that tall one? It's lit up at night," and he would describe it. "That's the only thing I can see of Arabella, of the outside world."

Some guards were decent, acting not kindly or compassionately but just normally. They treated the inmates like they were human. There were mean guards who regarded the inmates as subhuman or people who deserved lousy treatment. One of this ilk was the one who taunted Ahmed when he was working in the kitchen. He wanted extra food, which Ahmed was not allowed to give. When he said no, they strip-searched him coming and going into the kitchen. I think this went on for weeks. I mentioned it to the lawyer, but it didn't seem that there was much that he could do for fear that it would make matters even worse. But the strip-searches were a great indignity to Ahmed.

Dealing with the guards was hard, but dealing with the other inmates was challenging, too. Maybe about thirty percent of them were mentally ill. When they would come in, if they were not mentally ill, they were often strung out on drugs. Sometimes they were suffering from a combination of addictions and mental illness. There would be a lot of screaming during the night, all night long, and it made it challenging for Ahmed and others to get to sleep.

All the inmates I talked to said they had way too much time to think and worry. This was a constant complaint. They did not have enough to keep themselves busy, so their minds would start running in circles with worry and fear, and they did not know how to turn it off and relax.

In terms of trying to get some recreation to unwind, there was only one newspaper for the whole *mod* of thirty guys. Ahmed never tried to get the newspaper. That was impossible.

Some inmates attempted to pass the time with artsy things that required some form of paint, which they would make. They would get colors from colored gummy bears, or somehow they would add deodorant to colorful ads in the newspapers. They could get some color off the ink and use that to do their paintings and artwork.

There was not much available in the library but novels. I have yet to hear much else from Ahmed about that. He loved reading self-help books, especially the one titled *Happy Anywhere*. He read that book and others over and over again. Some were given to him by friends he made in jail. Reading these books helped him bolster his positivity and gratitude and made him a role model for others. Those books were just part of a program of foundational behavioral reinforcement: "This is how I want to be, and this is how I want to feel, despite everything that's going on around me."

One teacher employed by the county was trying to help the inmates get their GEDs. Four inmates started with Ahmed but dropped out of the classes, leaving Ahmed as the only one. He tried to work hard on his studies. He never passed any of the exams. It was tough to study with so many distractions during the day. There were only a few feet between his rack of three beds and the next rack of three beds, so the distractions were frequent and loud, and there was no personal space to sit and have a quiet place to study.

There was a "God mod" where several inmates went to celebrate and have a religious experience, but he did not attend those. He said the way the inmates would act after, outside of, those gatherings did not impress him. He thought it was very hypocritical what was going on. But anyway, that was his reasoning.

One privilege Ahmed enjoyed was choosing the shower he wanted. He had been there the longest, and it was customary for the longest in jail to choose first. In the bathrooms and elsewhere, there was a lot of sneezing, coughing, and farting. There was just no sense of embarrassment. The guys were out of it, did not care, or were proud of it, and so the place was not only noisy but smelly at the same time.

They got some pretty decent haircuts there. One guy from the jail was a barber. But in terms of other personal things, they gave out toothbrushes, which were awful. They were short-handled and wimpy and almost useless. However, they did get soap and shampoo.

Ahmed was always attentive to the mail and the mail call. He did this because if a guard were not paying attention or did not like you, they would not call you for mail. The schedule for when he would be called down to see me was something he knew. He paid close attention so that if no one called him to say the mail was here or no one called to say, "It is time to go downstairs; somebody is waiting," he would be up there and check on them and say, "Didn't I get called to come down? I must have been called," or "I must have been called to get my mail."

Ahmed was always easy to talk to. He was open, extremely articulate, and sincere, and he trusted me from the beginning. Our time was always way too short because there was so much that he wanted to talk about. He spoke most of the time, which was appropriate, and partly because of AIDVP, I was not supposed to be talking about myself, not to be talking about my family. Occasionally, I would say a little about myself so that he knew I also trusted him.

His strengths were just unbelievable, and that is what I tried to draw out from him in this sad place of many challenges. And so I helped him focus on his gifts: his compassion, the things he had been able to do, and his survival skills. He could show weakness to me, but he could not show it out there. Out there, you show it, and you know they can capitalize on that. He would take newcomers under his wing, listen to them, and help them feel understood, but he always stood his ground and let people know he could defend himself. So when he came in to visit with me, he could be disarmed, tell the truth about his feelings, and say anything he wanted, and it was a very blessed time for him and me.

13

Why Are You Here?

> Your cold blood cannot be worked into a fever; your veins are full of ice water; but mine are boiling, and the sight of such chillness makes them dance.
>
> —Emily Brontë, *Wuthering Heights*

Lucy

Annie is my very good friend. I marveled at her weekly dedication to visit a Somali refugee in jail. And not only that, but she was also helping Ahmed with a lawyer. After several months, I asked her, "Besides helping financially, what else can I do?"

"Why don't you come with me to the hearing," Annie said. "It's Ahmed's second court hearing."

And I agreed. So after a security check, I entered a tiny courtroom—a couple of rows for people in the public to sit and upfront, just a couple of desks, a plaintiff table, a defense table, and a simple judge's bench for the immigration judge. This was the first time I saw Ahmed, but I wasn't allowed to speak with him.

As I walked in, there was a look of annoyance on the prosecutor's face. And the judge seemed startled a bit, like, what are other people doing here? The prosecutor looked up at me. "Why are you here?" she said.

"I thought it was a public hearing," I said.

There was a pause while the prosecutor considered this and checked me out from head to toe. Then there was some quiet discussion between the prosecutor and the judge. "Please be seated," the judge declared and returned to what she was doing.

Annie was there already. She was also present at the hearing before this one. They knew her as Ahmed's sponsor.

I was there as a witness, a friend of Annie's from our faith group. I had no legal experience. What help could I be? But I was there as a body, a presence, to be there for Annie's friend. To let Ahmed know other people cared about him.

What I observed about Ahmed was that he was handcuffed. That surprised me just to see a man handcuffed in a courtroom. I don't think that's common unless we're talking about a truly dangerous criminal.

I could not help but notice his smile. It communicated appreciation and respect. When I took my seat in the courtroom, he looked at me and nodded as a friend would even though we had never met. I had never seen him in jail, so this was the one day I could see him face-to-face. And here was a man on trial for seeking asylum, and a total stranger walked in. He knew nothing about me other than what Annie told him, and he just looked up and smiled with such gratitude. It was like we bowed to each other and were instantly bonded, and I do not know how else to describe that.

I found him amazingly calm in that hearing, which settled my nervousness. I learned much about his story because the prosecutor asked him many questions, and Ahmed confidently answered them.

As I sat there, I was in awe at what he had been through—being nearly killed, fleeing his homeland, and saying goodbye to his family—and what he had to do to get a smuggler, a stranger, to move him from place to place like some baggage. He would have been put on airplanes and buses and traveled with strangers in cars, with no say at all. And as for me, I never even considered that. I could go anywhere in the world that I wanted to. And I heard his story about landing in Central America, making it through Mexico, and getting to the border, where several authorities questioned him quite a few times.

I was amazed at his composure because the prosecutor repeatedly confronted him: "You lied about this," and, "You lied about that." And he would come right out and say, "When you're being smuggled, you have to say what you need to say." And I think that challenged his integrity to say whatever a smuggler directed him to speak because his life was in danger. His life was in the smuggler's hands. His was a choice of openness or survival.

I was stunned by the prosecutor, how cold she was. And there was no sense in what she conveyed that she was speaking to an innocent man. There before her was a man who had committed no crime against the United States, yet he sat in handcuffs, and she treated him just as if he had been on trial for murder. It left a terrible taste in my mouth, for, oh my god, if this is what happens to him, what happens to people who have made a dreadful mistake, done something wrong, something criminal? The coldness she revealed, the seeming lack of human respect—I swear a smile would have cracked her face. She was fighting against him, and I don't know why. That just bothered me so much. I understand she was a prosecutor who had to lay out facts and make a case, but I will not forget that feeling of disrespect.

But most of all, I was taken with Ahmed's smile under pressure and his sincerity in telling his story. He was serene. He would not let her get to him.

When the hearing ended, I had not understood all of it, but I knew from across the room that he was grateful that I was there. Someday, we would be able to meet. We would.

It was wrong for him to be in handcuffs and controlled like that. As he was escorted out the door, I felt a powerful sense of injustice that he was restrained like that, but I didn't know what to do about it, and I thank God that Annie and Ahmed's attorney were already working on securing his freedom. Still, I helplessly asked what I could do. This was so unjust.

Annie

May 10, 2017
Hello Ahmed!

Well, I'm back in jail—so to speak. All is forgiven for my mistake. I expect to visit you at the usual time next week, May 16.

The Tuesday court hearing went smoothly. I was surprised to learn that you and Zoya had obtained more evidence helpful to your case. Warren thought he had sent me this info, but he had not. I was delighted and relieved to discover this in a conversation with him *after* the hearing was over. It will undoubtedly bolster your case. With the new evidence, I hope the case will go well, and you'll be closer to home.

Stay well—in God's peace and time.

Annie

On that next Tuesday, I had a pleasant conversation with Ahmed. He said he was happy to see me and seemed very relaxed and content. He had a way of tuning out all that was happening around him in the jail and being very present to me during our one hour of conversation. "You met lots of interesting people in jail," I said. "One of them was the cook. Could you tell me more about him?"

"You're referring to Doug, the gentleman that was working in the kitchen?" Ahmed asked.

"Yes."

"Okay, let me talk about him. A little before I met you, as you know, they promoted me to trustee. I had more freedom and found a job in the kitchen. I started earning forty cents an hour, three dollars a day, and twenty dollars a week. They put me on the p.m. shift, and my main job was to cater for the dinner. Doug is the person in charge and the head chef. He is an African American veteran and retired soldier who works for a food service company that supplies the jail.

"He is my boss and one of the kindest persons I have come to know in the jail. He makes sure that he cooks special food for the twenty-one of us, twenty-one crew members on that shift. Hot stuff like jalapenos or chili is something he knows I like. And he buys special food from his own pocket almost every day for the entire week that he cooks, food that you normally would not get in jail. He has often called me over and told me, 'Look at this. This is what you are going to eat tonight.'"

"Does he treat the other crew members as well as you?" I asked.

"Yes. He became like a father figure to me and to all of us. It is like he is cooking in his own house for the entire jail. Every day, he would, you know, cook from his heart. He is very kind. One time, one of the crew members was caught eating food he had taken from the kitchen. The security guard told us, 'Tonight, you're all going to get only a single tray.'

"But Doug negotiated with him, 'Hey, don't do that. These people are just inmates. This is the only thing they have. And besides, I'm not throwing good food away.'

"Doug has strong values, so everyone has come to respect him."

"What did you mean when you said, 'Only a single tray'?"

"If one of us makes a mistake, for example, we would all be punished. Getting only a single tray means there was nothing special for the crew. We'd get a single tray like all the other inmates."

"Ah, I see."

"I have some special memories of working with Doug. He was always the one standing behind the table to dish out the food. He knew what I liked, and he would sometimes give me more. And during the fasting time of Ramadan, special food was not allowed by the rules, but he would buy the special food anyway and place it underneath some rice. And on top, he would put the fries or other food that all the inmates were getting. And that's how I got my Ramadan food while working. I could not eat it then, but I saved it for later that evening, after sunset."

"I can see why the kitchen crew likes him. He is very considerate, very caring," I said.

"Absolutely. Sometimes he would bring a can of pop, like a Coke or a Pepsi, which is a big deal when you are an inmate. So he would open the pop, call three or four of us, and tell us to share it. To drink that little bit of, you know, just two or three sips of pop was a special treat that you would talk about for days. But he would do that for us."

"Wow. Yeah. He knows what you are experiencing. He knows how hard it is."

"Absolutely. He knows what we are going through, and he knows that a few of us are immigrants. He is a tough guy but has a very caring heart. He wouldn't like to see us suffering. I mean, you could see the kindness in his heart. Everybody liked him. He was like a father figure."

> May 18, 2017
> Hello Ahmed!
>
> Well, it seems things are returning to normal after some bumpy, emotional days.
>
> Be proud of all you have accomplished toward your GED degree. Your internal discipline is a powerful asset for achieving long-term goals and handling the low times.
>
> By the way, Martin did try to come and see you when I was gone. He didn't know they had a new system in place where visitors had to register online and be cleared, so he wasn't allowed in.
>
> Greetings to Zoya and the children. I'll see you next week. Remember, if something comes up—like I get sick, an emergency, or the Pope drops by—there is no way I can let you know. I just wouldn't show up at the jail. If that should ever happen, just take it in stride. I'd let you know what happened in the following letter.
>
> Peace, my friend, until Tuesday.
>
> Annie

14

One Foot in the Doorway

> But Hope
> smiles from the threshold of the year to come,
> whispering, "It will be happier."
>
> —Alfred Lord Tennyson, *The Foresters* (1892)

Michael

When the immigration judge held her second hearing in early May, the purpose was to investigate further the "resettlement in South Africa" issue. Judge Helen had ruled on that in the first hearing with a statement only—she neglected to put her fact-finding and analysis in writing. This time would be different.

Ahmed gave testimony under oath at the hearing:

- He went to South Africa on May 5, 1997.
- He did not leave South Africa until he returned to Somalia in March of 2016.
- He was never granted permanent residency in South Africa and only had an "asylum seeker temporary permit," which was subject to continual renewal.
- Temporary residence in South Africa did not lead to permanent residency.

- When his life was threatened in 2010, he gave money to a smuggler to get him out of South Africa, but he did not leave.
- He had at one time given his personal information to a smuggler: his name, his date of birth, and a picture.

There were many other things Ahmed told the judge under oath. There were also multiple documents accepted as evidence to corroborate his testimony. Much of what he said contradicted what was in the documents of exhibits 7 and 8.

When Judge Alexander wrote up her decision, she devoted nearly half of the document to Ahmed's testimony. She addressed credibility again. The judge emphasized its extreme importance to the case and how the court must make a "threshold credibility determination" but did not divulge what criteria she used or what the threshold was.

Next, the judge discussed "Firm Resettlement—Law and Analysis." In this three-page section, she stated the various parts of the law concerning firm resettlement and compared them one by one with the testimony and evidence provided by Ahmed. The judge found that firm resettlement, as defined in the law, did not apply to Ahmed's case. The reasons given were "inconsistencies and inaccuracies" in the evidence provided by DHS. The evidence did not point to an offer that Ahmed could indefinitely remain in South Africa or one day could achieve permanent residency there.

On June 6, 2017, Helen Alexander signed the judge's decision. This was the second time the judge granted asylum to Ahmed.

Annie

Emails: June 6, 2017
Subject: Congrats on the Decision

[Annie to Warren]

Congratulations on the positive outcome from the Judge. You did a marvelous job representing Ahmed! I expect you will receive the judge's written decision before long. I'd love to read it.

Will DHS likely declare early on if they are contesting, or will we just find out sometime before July 5 when/if they submit their documents? July 4 will have a whole new meaning this year if they don't appeal.

P.S. I see Ahmed at 1:00 today.

[Warren to Annie]

I'm at court, but Ahmed called and told my staff—that's excellent news! The decision might get sent to my old address, so it may be a few days before I receive it. I will forward it once I receive it.

However, I will reach out to the Govt and try to convince them not to appeal, although that might be a long shot given their hellbent intention to pursue deportation at all costs. They should tell me and [must] put me on notice by sending me a copy of any notice of appeal they filed with the Board of Immigration Appeals.

The next day, Warren sent the judge's written decision to Annie.

[Warren to Annie]

Here it is. The credibility finding was vital, as was finding the Government's letter unreliable. I'm still working on finding out whether the

Government [DHS] will appeal again. I'll be in touch when I know more.

June 21, 2017
Good morning, Ahmed!

    Happy End of Ramadan—*Eid al-Fitr*. I know this is a big deal back home and will probably be a big deal for the small community of Muslims celebrating together in the jail. Honor the moment, Ahmed. I bet you will remember this place and time of Ramadan forever.

Annie

July 5, 2017
Good morning, Ahmed!

    I'm just settling in with the expected news that DHS is *again* appealing the Arabella judge's favorable ruling giving you asylum. Trump's administration is hell-bent on keeping Somali nationals out, as are some members of the DHS prosecution in Arabella. I am confident the preponderance of the evidence submitted in the May hearing answering the single open question will finally set you free.
    So, hang in there. Your home team did a great job supplying evidence that Warren professionally submitted to the court. All has been done that can be done and done well.

Annie

July 13, 2017
Hello Ahmed!

Thanks for the great visit last week. You *are* making progress toward that goal of release, being set free after two favorable asylum rulings by the Arabella judge. I pray for Zoya that this challenging time will bring strength and resources she never thought she had.

I have not had a response back yet from your lawyer regarding 1) the best-case time scenario for resettling your family here, 2) if you could now get out on bond since DHS is no longer contesting your country status, and 3) the ongoing issue you described in our conversation [strip-searches].

Don't lose heart, Ahmed! Something is going to shake loose. Maybe your lawyer will convince the BIA that the prosecution's current appeal is bogus—wasting everyone's time and taxpayer money. Perhaps he's working on some sort of release. There is a saying, "Be patient toward all that is unsettled in your heart and try to love the questions themselves." That's a tall order. But that is the nature and invitation of mystery, especially when it involves family—those we cherish the most.

Peace,
Annie

Emails: July 12–15, 2017
Subject: Ahmed, litigation

[Annie to Warren]

Ahmed tells me that DHS's appeal papers have come through. I know you'll be sending me more info on that soon. As you do, here are a couple of things on my mind:

If DHS's appeal no longer stands on the question of his resettlement or nationality but rather something wonky like country conditions in Somalia, is Ahmed now eligible for bond/bail while Virginia reviews the appeal again? Getting out would significantly reduce pressure on him and the family.

In the best-case scenario, how long does it take to bring the *family* of an official asylee to the States? His wife is not doing well, and he's figuring well over a year.

Kitchen workers like Ahmed have been strip-searched about every other day for two months. One guard is getting perverse pleasure doing this, which is very demoralizing to the inmates. No one says anything, fearing it will make things worse. What are your thoughts on this?

[Warren to Annie]

I have more information now as I've received DHS's notice of appeal. I've spoken to Ahmed about this. While they could argue differently later on, from the brief's position set forth in their notice of appeal, it seems as if they might be conceding the firm resettlement issue and are just disputing that Ahmed suffered persecution and was credible. In other words, it's just as we suspected. I'll be ready to argue that the judge already decided this issue—and was not disturbed by the board of immigration appeals—so there's no need to relitigate it now. Still, I'll also have to reiterate how it was persecution, and he was credible, just to play it safe. It's a shame DHS keeps fighting this, but it is what it is. As a result, I will have to charge another $2,000 to complete this.

He's not eligible for bond, but ICE could release him if they want. I'll keep pushing for this, but it's highly unlikely. Fortunately, this second appeal should be decided within a few months.

Ahmed can petition for his wife and children if the appeal is dismissed. Even though they are Somali, Trump's travel ban doesn't apply because of their close family relationship. However, this could indeed take nine months to a year.

[Annie to Warren]

Thanks for your thorough note.

It's a shame for Ahmed, the family, and the taxpayers that they keep changing their arguments to different issues. But as you say, it is what we expected. Please go ahead and keep fighting. All of us are hoping this is the last round in the fight for asylum. I'll get a check to you soon.

Regarding bond and eligibility for release, I thought they held him, arguing that his country of origin wasn't established. I mean, what the heck kind of danger is he to anyone? And why would he want to flee, given that he is so close to getting asylum? Thanks for pushing for the possibility of release.

Nine months to a year for his family to join him is a better timeframe than I expected.

Yes, Ahmed has experienced the strip-search treatment from the guard for several months. I believe all the inmates/detainees working in the kitchen have. Ahmed is concerned that the guards will really come down on him if any report about this gets associated with his name. He's already considering quitting the kitchen job because that issue is hard to bear. But the job supplies income for calling his family. I trust you have ways of conveying information that doesn't single out who reported it.

[Warren to Annie]

Yes, it's disingenuous to hold him based on the lack of establishing his identity, and yet now it seems [ICE wants] to keep holding him despite not continuing to make that argument. I'm going straight to the top on this one.

As for the guard situation, perhaps we should wait until Ahmed is released to play it safe. I need to get as many details as possible from Ahmed before I raise it with the jail administrator.

[Annie to Warren]

YES! Thank you for going to the top. There is no reason to hold him. You have all my prayers at your back, Warren. Go for it!

I agree about the jail situation. We're so close, and playing it safe for now makes sense.

Emails: July 14, 2017
Subject: Ahmed, litigation

[Annie to Charlie and Marie]

Hi Charlie and Marie! It won't be long before the girls are back from camp. And the house will be rocking and rolling with their energy again. We missed them and got off a couple of letters to both.

We are wondering if you would like to contribute to what we believe will be the final round of litigation to set Ahmed free. You can see why so many asylee families give up. Without funds and a lawyer, DHS will take you down even when your case is perfect. People just wear out financially, emotionally, and physically—on all fronts.

The lawyer's report is below. You can opt out of this at any time. We trust you will be honest about your feelings. But we also want to extend the invitation if this is a fight you want to be a part of.

[Charlie to Annie]

Yes, we're looking forward to seeing the girls tomorrow!

Marie and I talked it over, and we'd be up for covering 2/3 of the expenses if you or others could cover the other 1/3. Here's hoping there's a light at the end of this struggle for Ahmed.

15

Intimidation

> There is a stubbornness about me that never can bear to be frightened at the will of others. My courage always rises at every attempt to intimidate me.
>
> —Jane Austen, *Pride and Prejudice*

Annie

July 20, 2017
Hello there Ahmed!

    I haven't heard anything back from Warren regarding a potential release for you while litigation goes forward. I'll contact him if there is still no word by Monday.
    I'm volunteering this weekend at an event with Warren where immigrants and asylees come to get help to apply for a green card. I should learn a lot. I might just be assigned to be a greeter, but that will be inspiring in any case.

Peace and blessings,
Annie

REFUGEE ON THE THRESHOLD

Emails: July 22–24, 2017
Subject: Potential Release and $

[Annie to Warren]

Any news regarding Ahmed's release? Is DHS still fighting it? I walked your check ($2,000) down to the mailbox this morning.

[Warren to Annie]

I spoke with the head government attorney in Arabella last week. He indicated that it was a joint decision (with the trial attorney) to appeal because they didn't think the judge applied the law correctly. He also mentioned it was because the judge was new. So it's about intimidation, which is ridiculous and not exactly the most ethical tactic, but they often do it.

I'm also waiting to hear back on *release*, so I'll be in touch about that when I hear back.

[Annie to Warren]

So, the head Arabella Gov't attorney agreed with the trial attorney that the judge misapplied the law. This has got me worried. What part of the law are they zeroing in on for the argument?

Maybe it's because it's so late, but these folks are starting to wear me down. It feels like they could keep shifting focus and go on appealing *something* indefinitely. I don't think Ahmed or I could go another round. Perhaps I am being overly dramatic? Is there a real cause for concern? I thought litigation was almost over.

And we'll hope they reply positively about his release.

[Warren to Annie]

I don't have their latest brief yet, but I believe the focus will be on credibility and persecution, on which the judge agreed with us, which is huge, as the Gov't burden to overcome is very high.

But you hit the nail on the head. You don't get multiple shots at appealing the same issue(s), which will be one of the arguments I lead with. They appealed all issues the first time, and the case was remanded only for the firm resettlement issue. The Board of Immigration Appeals reviews all issues *de novo*—in the first instance—and mentioned all of the Government's arguments in their first decision but only mentioned one reason for the remand. That was disposed of in our favor as well, of course. If the Board had issues with Ahmed's credibility and/or persecution, they would have said so and remanded accordingly to address all issues.

I know this is frustrating, and it's easy for me to say, but I truly think the Board will agree with us.

*****

REFUGEE ON THE THRESHOLD

August 9, 2017
Hello Ahmed,

 A lovely visit, as always. I appreciate learning more about your family, especially about the cultures and events that have shaped all of you. I have so much respect for you and Zoya—with all that life has thrown at you—you have modeled how to be courageous and honorable for your children. You live without bitterness and hatred when it would be easy to go down those destructive avenues. Zoya might be stuck in a small apartment in South Africa, but she is the domestic version of Rambo. How many women could do what she is doing and withstand long-term danger, stress, and separation? You two are a good match, and your commitment to each other is an example for us all.
 There is a grocery store chain called ALDI. It's a store that limits its inventory to only a few choices of items. Prices are generally from 25 to 30% cheaper than alternative stores. I will introduce you to this place when you get out. It's great for saving money. It might also be an excellent place to work. People returning from life in Africa to the States are often overwhelmed by the sheer number of choices here.
 It will be an adventure when you are released. For now, you are doing all you can, preparing internally and spiritually, taking care of your family, and studying for the time when you are released. All kinds of doors will be opened, and you, Zoya, and the kids will explore a whole new world.

Peace,
Annie

August 23, 2017
Good morning, Ahmed,

    Warren sent a very encouraging email today, saying he believes your case will be over in a few months. He is very optimistic. I remain so as well.

    All those driving skills are going to come in very handy. You'll want independence for traveling to work, the Mosque, the grocery store, and some entertainment. As each of these things becomes more real for you, the reality of a coming new life will also become more real for Zoya. Your freedom to move around, work, worship, make friends, and get out into nature will become her hope, her mirror, as will your freedom to call her anytime, each of you with a cup of tea as you talk about the small things in life.

    Time to get my act together and have a morning cup of coffee. The household is asleep. Husby was up late watching some action/adventure film where the good guys beat the crap out of the bad guys, and life has a tidy, satisfying ending. We all need our illusions.

    I wish you peace and deep consolation.

Annie

Sept 6, 2017
Hello Ahmed!

    Thanks for the great visit today and for the touching stories about your compassionate grandmother, mother, and auntie. One day you will gift your grandchildren these stories and stories about your incredible sister, Fawzia. These women of your family excel in courage, tenderness, mentoring, and love!

Thanks, too, for the description of childhood courage—you were surviving a massive helicopter attack and a blanket of bullets by hiding in a culvert with a bunch of terrifying critters.

I wish you moments of deep peace and sustaining memories of courage and the amazing people who lived it.

Annie

Michael

DHS was determined to keep fighting. Since the judge had successfully answered the question of firm resettlement in South Africa, DHS let go of that issue but essentially repeated all the other arguments made in their first appeal. But the BIA did not mention any of these additional arguments in their reason for remand.

I was quite optimistic that the BIA would not look at these arguments for a second time but uphold the second ruling for asylum and deny DHS's appeal. This outcome seemed only logical to Warren Jackson, an immigration attorney with lots of experience, and I relied on him to get a sense of the case.

On September 7, 2017, DHS and respondent submitted their appeal briefs to the BIA. In "Respondent's Brief in Opposition to DHS's Second Appeal," Attorney Jackson argued (1) the DHS counselor raised no new issue in this second appeal, (2) the immigration judge did not make an error in her assessment of firm resettlement, and (3) the immigration judge correctly found updated country conditions in Somalia continued to support Ahmed's eligibility for asylum.

Warren's arguments were further developed by statements of the facts, statements pertaining to immigration law, and citations of precedent. In the briefs on appeal that Warren submitted to the BIA, he saw his role as supporting the rulings of the judge. But the board, in its declarations concerning the appeals by DHS, restated the arguments of DHS like they were irrefutable, and never once did the BIA or DHS mention any counter-arguments by Atty. Warren Jackson. There was no documentation by either BIA or DHS to support that an immigrant attorney even existed. Other than in the header of their documents, I could not find one example.

Now that we were waiting for the results of the second appeal, would anything be different this time? Would the BIA show they had received a convincing argument from the attorney for Ahmed? And would they rule for asylum (deny DHS's appeal)?

September 12 marks the one-year anniversary of Annie's first meeting with Ahmed, but Annie was continuing her week-by-week visits and following up with encouraging letters. I felt my job was to continue encouraging Annie. And we waited, and we waited some more.

Annie

September 13, 2017
Hello Ahmed!

There never seems to be enough time in the short visiting window. But we pack in as much as we can. I sent a note to Martin about visiting hours that work best for you, along with your renewed apologies for the roadblocks he hit. This should solve the problem.

After you get asylee status and are released, there will be members of our Christian community to help.

I hope the book on computer coding will give you a peek into what kind of work this field involves. Admittedly, reading a book is a narrow perspective, but it's better than a total guess. There are so many jobs in the computer field, but many involve years of education to get started. This field might be easier to crack. Often, if one gets a job with an employer, the company will pay for an education that helps the individual improve in the work they are currently doing in the company. These larger companies want to strengthen the employees' skill levels.

Well, now I've got to go out and seal the concrete. The winters are harsh here. Water, snow, and ice get into cracks and damage even concrete. Sealants and calking help protect and close surfaces. So that's the task for today.

See you soon.

Annie

October 4, 2017
Hello Ahmed!

So lovely visiting with you again today, seeing the significant progress on your Language Arts section of the GED, hearing about your family, catching up on your work situation, and making plans for your release.

Once you receive asylee's status, [Zoya] will have a significant role in getting the family ready to travel. Warren says you would file a form I-730 for a V-92 visa for your family. A US Government website says V-92 beneficiaries will need to provide an *original and a photocopy* of the following civil documents for each beneficiary (as applicable) to prove identity and relationship to you, the petitioner:

- Birth certificate
- Marriage certificate

- Six photographs of each beneficiary
- Photocopy of the biographical data page of the beneficiary's passport, if available
- A certified English translation must accompany documents written in a language other than English

During the interview, beneficiaries may be asked to supply the following:

- A passport not due to expire at least six months beyond the intended entry into the USA or a picture identification card such as a refugee travel document
- Other evidence of the relationship between the family and petitioner (you), such as photographs, school records, family correspondence, phone bills, documentation of financial support
- A Medical Exam report which an embassy-approved panel will provide after the completion of the exam and vaccinations. *Follow-to-join asylees* (as opposed to *follow-to-join refugees*) are responsible for paying the cost of this exam

Warren can help with this process. He didn't provide this list, but U.S. government websites are usually reliable.

May this time of expectation deepen your peace and trust in God in a way you never dreamed possible. That would be, ironically, a priceless and soul-freeing gift from the ugly confines of a jail.

See you Tuesday.

Annie

October 12, 2017
Hello Ahmed!

I called the court hotline yesterday, and nothing was happening. I think it might take six weeks in Virginia for the BIA to decide. I don't know why. I've just got that stuck in my head. It is such a hectic time, this waiting.

I called the Department of Motor Vehicles today. They are sending out the Iowa Drivers Manual to you today. It could be a nice distraction in jail if things drag on. They have practice tests online, too, for when you get out.

Annie

Email: October 17, 2017
Subject: Contact info for O'Malley family—upon Ahmed's Release

[Annie to Warren]

We are counting down the days until Ahmed's release and your call or email to say he is free! Ahmed was in high spirits today when I visited. He says his only request upon release will be to sleep for 24 hours. Apparently, it is tough to rest in jail.

Below is the contact information for the O'Malley family, who will take in Ahmed upon his immediate release if we are in California. We will be there for two weeks. We leave tomorrow. When the word comes down, contact Martin or Kate, and let them know where to go; one of them will hop right over to wherever they need to be. Michael will return from California when Ahmed is released, but that might take a day or so.

I hope you celebrate every victory you work so hard to bring about. Every family you keep together and every family you keep from harm. Each victory bends the arc of history in someone's family tree. God willing, in Ahmed's case, there will always be "before" America and "after." That's an awesome thing.

Attachment: Contact Info for O'Malley, Martin and Kate; Michael and Annie.

*****

November 8, 2017
Hello there, Ahmed!

I am so grateful that Zoya is recovering from the car accident without much pain or doctor's bills. I hope she will have a smile on her face and feel a lot better by Friday. And I am happy, too, that you were able to talk to your children, who miss you so much. You are a wonderful and caring father. I know that all you are going through is an effort to make life better for your whole family. They, indeed, are what this entire ordeal is about.

I sure hope this letter gets through. I write one *every* week, and if they continue to get lost in the mail on the way to you, I'll contact the jail to see if I'm doing something wrong or if there is a hold-up some place. Quite a few letters seem to have gone missing. That makes me sad. And curious as to what's happening…Continue to hang tough, my friend.

Peace,
Annie

November 17, 2017
Good morning, Ahmed,

Thank you for the great visit yesterday! Your positive energy was catchy, and the good news that letters are coming through again made me smile.

Breaking down barriers is often the work and strength of the succeeding generations. You have generously shared stories about what happened as you challenged Somalia's cultural, national, and religious identities. That's one *really* hard row to hoe. People die crossing those lines. Your children will reap the benefits of mom and dad challenging the bigotry and discrimination that comes with ignorance and fear. You have challenged that cruel legacy with courage, love, grace, and forgiveness.

I look forward to seeing you again this coming Tuesday.

Peace,
Annie

November 21, 2017
Hello Ahmed!

    Thanks for the wonderful visit today and the update on what's happening in the facility. I am pleased that they are remodeling (and adding on to?) the jail. It's stressful for everyone, including staff, when a facility is in horrible shape and inmates are severely overcrowded.

    Tomorrow, we will have a Thanksgiving meal with our daughter. On Thursday, we will celebrate with Lucy and Bill's family. So there will be much feasting on fancy, fattening foods while recalling the year's blessings. I forgot to ask if inmates in the jail will have anything special for their Thanksgiving meal. I sure hope so. Will you have a part in that?

    The AIDVP coordinator checked with the jail program coordinator about the mail. She found out that mail monitors in the jail do not read what they open. They only open letters, tip everything out, and check for additional items, like smuggled drugs.

    One of the individuals in our family who is mentally disabled gets excited about Thanksgiving. Every year we recite the "Litany of the Turkey." He phones, and we go down the list of who is bringing what to the Thanksgiving meal. It's been pretty much the same list since 1986. But he needs to go through the ritual of matching names and food. [And when I ask,] "Who will bring Apple Pie?"—"ME," he will say. And maybe flowers for the table.

Peace,
Annie

16

Nexus

In the final analysis, true justice is not a matter of courts and law books, but of a commitment in each of us to liberty and mutual respect.

—Jimmy Carter

Michael

On November 30, 2017, the BIA again remanded the case for further proceedings. Tacitly taking up DHS's arguments and with reference only to the judge's written decision, the BIA made the following points to back up their decision to remand the case:

- The BIA found *clear error* in the immigration judge's determination that Ahmed established the required *nexus* (connection) between the threats he received and a protected ground, as the decisions of the immigration judge appeared to show such nexus was that of nationality.
- The board found that Ahmed's political opinion claim was speculative and lacked substantial analysis by the judge, so the board instructed the immigration judge to reevaluate her nexus finding.

- The board requested the immigration judge to consider DHS's arguments regarding Ahmed's credibility.
- The BIA asked the judge to determine if Ahmed qualified for relief under the Convention Against Torture (CAT).

This remand by the board was an appalling and thoroughly discouraging ruling. It meant that the BIA had brushed aside the purpose of their first remand (firm resettlement) to revisit the judge's first decision for asylum.

I felt that now that the first remand was sufficiently answered, the BIA was not happy. They were making this a competition. But what they were involved in deciding, and had the last word, was not trivial. It was a matter of life or death for Ahmed.

Annie

December 4, 2017
Hello Ahmed,

Sometimes, I feel like we have run the Boston marathon only to look down and find we're still at the starting gate.

Or not. Nobody's sure yet, but we'll find out in a few days. I've been praying for you as we hold our collective breath, waiting to learn more about the latest BIA ruling from Virginia. I don't know about you, but when I got the update from Warren on Sunday, I had a slump day, giving sadness, fear, and anger some space.

Please send my warmest greetings to Zoya and the children.

Annie

Emails: December 11–14, 2017
Subject: Anything to pass on?

[Annie to Warren]

I'll see Ahmed tomorrow at 1:00. Any news you'd like me to pass on? He will ask if I've heard anything or if you have any feelings about what is coming down.

[Warren to Annie]

I did just get a copy of the BIA remand decision. It is attached along with the December 2016 Immigration Judge's decision referenced in it. As you can probably see, the Immigration Judge determined that Ahmed was a member of a particular social group because of his Ashraf clan (she spends nearly a whole page in her decision on it) but then failed to mention that he was persecuted on account of it on the next page which the BIA ran with. This was an innocent omission that I thought the BIA would be able to understand, but they did not and ignored this altogether, although they can review everything in the first instance.

The judge and BIA also didn't explain the political opinion (Al-Shabaab targeted him because he was applying at a government hospital, and Al-Shabaab hates the Somali government and those who support it and targets them accordingly) much because of the social group analysis [focus].

I'm extremely disappointed in this decision, which, of course, pales compared to the disappointment Ahmed will have.

Here's what we can do:

- File a motion to reconsider arguing the above. This would have to be received by 12/30. I would have to charge $1000 to do this. Or,
- Do nothing now and wait for the next hearing before the immigration judge. This will require a new trial and, of course, more money.

Either way, this will delay things. I know Ahmed may want to give up—and I can't blame him—but this judge wants to grant him asylum and, of course, has twice now. If she does it the right way this time—and I'll continue to lead her—this could solve everything once and for all. I plan on talking to Ahmed in person tomorrow afternoon as well, so please let him know.

Annie, I'll keep fighting this for as long as everyone wants me to.

[Annie to Warren]

Thanks for your reply. I am so glad you have an appointment to see Ahmed today. He received the papers at the end of November and has been stressed about their implications for the future. His family is also very worried. We discussed options as best we knew them so he would be more emotionally prepared for the conversation with you today. Ahmed described a possible option for "delayed deportation" (something I had never heard of), which would allow him to get out of jail and stay in the U.S.A. for some time before being deported. If this is a serious option, Michael and I could help prepare his way and send him to a 3-month website coding boot camp in the U.S.A., enabling him to get a decent job in Africa upon return. Somehow, I doubt the prosecution would let him out of jail.

We can find funds for ongoing attorney's fees. But we are concerned about how much more stress his family can take. Also, my confidence in winning another round of court hearings has taken a significant hit since this last appeal was supposed to be a done deal, and it wasn't. And there doesn't seem to be a sure-fire quick fix (unless option 1—the motion to reconsider—would do that).

Michael and I could schedule a conversation at your office if that were helpful to understand the pros/cons of possible approaches and what Ahmed wants to do. We leave for CA on Dec. 20th but are wide open before then.

Thanks so much for all your work helping Ahmed; I hope the conversation today was helpful for both of you.

[Warren to Annie]

Perhaps it would be easier to discuss this in person. I have some time available on Monday at 10 or 11 AM if that would work for you. He's been scheduled before the judge for 12/22, and I think it's best to just give this one more shot before the judge, due to her omissions on our strongest arguments. I can explain this (and my thinking) in more detail next week. The judge wants to grant him asylum and, in fact, has twice, but she just needs to clarify a few points, and I think the BIA will be satisfied.

December 14, 2017
Dear Ahmed,

    I am continually amazed at your courtesy, patience, and courage. When I visited, I had so much to say about what I had learned. You sat and listened and listened. And then I discovered that you knew all that I was relaying already. You had received the papers from the court many days earlier and had been dealing with their impact—*alone*—for all that time. Chee! Never once did you say, "Hold your horses there, Annie. We don't have much time, and I know most of that already." Nope. You patiently waited through all my "time-sensitive" news before you had a chance to open your heart. Thank you.

    I have been praying with more than one image lately. For about ten days, I would wake up with sadness and the image of a transparent, empty gift box with a pretty bow. I think my subconscious was saying: *There is nothing in the box. There is nothing to open. What you want is not there, Annie, no matter how pretty the bow.* But when I pray with the image, God assures me that the box is today's gift. And today is always a mystery. Today always holds a goodness to open. What that gift is, is not always apparent. Sometimes it is an opportunity—to give of myself to others rather than receiving what I want.

    Our family has a tradition whereby the older aunties sing a song at each wedding celebration to the newlywed couple. We sang that traditional song again to my nephew and his bride this year. Before we started, my oldest sister apologized for our missing members (some were sick) and our aging voices. We told *ourselves* that the gift of the song wasn't perfection. It wasn't to show us off. It conveyed how much the couple was loved and needed to love each other. And then we started to sing. And you know what, Ahmed? We nailed that song. We sang it loud and clear—the best we *ever* had. And when we finished, the roomful of primarily young people stood up and cheered and applauded. That moment is solid in my heart.

When I returned home, I found myself praying, gently holding my discouragement about your case, just sitting with my growing sadness. And then I heard the same lyrics, this time directed at me:

I'll walk in the rain by your side.
I'll cling to the warmth of your hand.
I'll do anything to help you understand
I love you more than anybody can.

—John Denver, *For Baby (For Bobbie)*

And that did it. That broke the sadness. I felt the truth Eternal Love wanted me to understand—a truth more important than anything else—how deeply I was loved. Not the outcome of your case. Not the answers. Not the roadmap. Just how profoundly I—and you—are valued.

So ended her short sermon.

Blessings,
Annie

Michael

Ahmed had been in jail now for a year and a half. The judge called another hearing, the third one in Ahmed's case, for December 22, 2017. She called it to gather additional verbal testimony from Ahmed. This hearing was only three weeks after the BIA remand (their second), and the holidays were imminent, so *briefs on remand* were not ordered due until January 11, 2018, to give each party time to present arguments before the court. Once Ahmed gave additional sworn testimony and Helen had read the briefs from Darcy and Warren, she would decide and put it in writing.

In his third brief sent to the judge, Attorney Jackson again stated the facts in the case, his arguments, and his conclusion. The brief was twenty-five pages long with an added sixty-five pages in one attachment, which contained updated country condition reports and news articles concerning Al-Shabaab. Warren's three arguments consisted of the following:

- The nexus of the respondent's past and future persecution is based upon his political opinion and/or his membership in a particular social group.
- Should the immigration judge determine the respondent is not eligible for asylum or withholding of removal, he seeks the alternative: relief under the Convention Against Torture (CAT).
- The immigration judge's favorable credibility finding should be upheld.

According to the first argument, Al-Shabaab targeted Ahmed based on his actual or imputed political opinion because of three reasons: Ahmed had applied for a government job, so he supported the government; he was married to an Ethiopian woman, so he had sided against Al-Shabaab in its war with Ethiopia; and he was a returning member of the Somalian diaspora, so he had left Somalia during the civil war instead of fighting for Al-Shabaab.

Country condition reports attached to the brief showed how lethal Al-Shabaab was in attacking anyone within Somalia who supported the government. Warren added facts concerning members of Ahmed's extended family to show how they were affected by Al-Shabaab. Ahmed's sister Fawzia, who had taken him into her home, was previously beaten by Al-Shabaab for listening to BBC radio. Ahmed's brother-in-law, Fawzia's husband, has since fled to an unknown location out of fear following the Al-Shabaab threat against Ahmed at his house. And two other brothers-in-law of Ahmed have also been killed by Al-Shabaab.

However, it remained that Al-Shabaab operatives had not spoken a word when they gave Ahmed the threat letter. And later that day, they told his sister, "He knows what to do." They did *not* say, "We know you support the Somali government, and we are here to threaten you." They did *not* say, "If you don't leave by tomorrow, we will come back to kill you." All of this was communicated implicitly in the letter, typed generically but delivered directly to him.

Although they had communicated with very few words, Ahmed knew well what they were saying. It was why he had gone on a dangerous journey and was now seeking asylum. And I reasoned anyone ought to see this, surely. They should decide this case in favor of Ahmed now, and he should be on his way to becoming an American citizen.

Warren made the second argument in his brief because the BIA had asked for findings from the judge concerning CAT, but the respondent's burden of proof was higher for CAT. There had to be at least a fifty-one percent chance he would be tortured or killed if returned to his home country. Only then would he qualify for relief, and the relief he would obtain could be temporary (deferring of removal), which might not lead to citizenship. But persecution on one of the five protected grounds was unnecessary. Ahmed's dependable testimony and Somalia's country conditions would be enough as long as Warren could prove that Somalia's government officials, while they were aware of the threat, would do nothing to intervene to prevent it being carried out.

The argument concerning CAT opened a whole other can of worms, and it would be seen whether the judge would argue for CAT or dismiss it because she favored the asylum claim.

In the third and last argument in Attorney Jackson's brief, Ahmed's credibility was examined once again. Warren took up two issues that DHS had used to discredit Ahmed's testimony. First, the black-flag symbol on the threat letter was not the official flag of Al-Shabaab—decorative and in color—as pictured in the country condition reports. But Warren argued that Al-Shabaab is also known to use a plain black flag as another identifying symbol.

Second, DHS alleged that Ahmed's testimony contained inconsistencies. But DHS was comparing Ahmed's testimony (under oath in Immigration Court) with notes taken by an asylum officer at his credible fear interview at the border. Warren argued that because the notes taken were not transcribed statements, were not sworn statements, and were not signed by Ahmed, they were unreliable, and on this, Warren referenced precedent.

In conclusion, Attorney Jackson summarized his arguments and asked that Ahmed's application for relief again be granted. *Would these sound arguments, if repeated in the upcoming ruling by the judge, be enough to convince the BIA?* I thought so.

17

The Last Straw

> The power of the lawyer is in the
> uncertainty of the law.
>
> —Jeremy Bentham

Annie

December 19, 2017
Hello Ahmed!

It seems you are settling into the new reality of another go-around in the courts. It's disappointing for sure, but I fully support your decision to stay the course. I am glad you are taking measures to reduce your stress.

I sent Warren an email that said you wanted to go forward in the courts and knew this would take some time to resolve.

Gosh, I'm *exhausted* tonight. And I am falling asleep here at my desk. But I wanted to get a little note off to you before I finish packing for the flight early tomorrow morning.

God bless you.

Annie

December 26, 2017
Greetings, my friend.

    Likely because of Christmas, I have not yet heard the results of last Friday's hearing from Warren. I don't know if you got a new court date or if anything significant happened. I am sure he will bring me up to speed soon.
    We went to the neighbor's house here in California for a celebration. They are from Romania. Their home was filled with *tall* family and friends speaking their mother tongue. I was so touched that the host and hostess made a point of making all of us feel welcome in their home. It was as if they were saying, "We know what it's like to be in a place where what you hear and see and taste is different. You belong here. And we care about you." I tried many of their Romanian dishes, which were outstanding.

Peace,
Annie

P.S. This will take longer to arrive as it has to get over the Rocky Mountains.

January 4, 2018
Hello Ahmed!

    A happy and Blessed New Year to you, my friend!…a new start. A new year. May it be a fantastic year for growth and progress in your case.

I'm back home now, and writing this letter is the first order of the day, having unpacked and put away a boatload of chocolate gifted to me by California friends of my son. Though I have told them repeatedly that I don't want or need any gifts, they feel they have to wrap up something.

You and your family were remembered, especially at New Year's Eve Mass, Ahmed. There is something so powerful about being with others who share the same values; even if the singing is minimal, people sit far apart because of colds and flu, and some are still half asleep. They show up. Their presence is a statement of what is essential and gives consolation to others gathered in the pews.

Today I will connect with Mandy again. As I have returned home, I have access to the information she needs to make first contact with Zoya. I can put names on each beautiful family face Warren forwarded to me. And I can provide phone, address, and email information as well. As it turns out, Mandy visited Johannesburg not long ago. She is enthused about this opportunity to begin a friendship and assist Zoya in this challenging time.

Mandy is a good person, optimistic, trained at Creighton University, very good in situations with multi-faith traditions, and knows how important it is to foster the individual's strengths.

I look forward to hearing what's been happening in the jail for the last two weeks. Perhaps you started writing in a journal? I think you mentioned that possibility. Your tales of conquest and woe, the craziness, repetition, and boredom—all that is outrageous, stupid, frustrating, unjust, and occasionally inspiring and grounding—it is all a small window into a world I would never otherwise know. And your description of it is a gift to me, whether or not it seems that way to you.

I also look forward to your description of the court hearing *without* an informed DHS person there to represent the prosecution and your take on how things went down.

Blessings,
Annie

January 10, 2018
Hello Ahmed!

What a delightful visit yesterday after not seeing you for three weeks! I was amazed to find you in such good spirits! Perhaps those simple extra comforts stashed in your locker add to your quality of life? And for sure, knowing your case is proceeding a bit more rapidly than we expected (at least at this point) is also a positive.

Tomorrow the briefs are due, and we will all know a bit more about what the prosecution has in theirs this time. Hopefully, there will be nothing new, and your verbal testimony, along with further signed affidavits, will finally settle any points of the prosecution and the remand request from Virginia [BIA].

I will be writing to Martin today to send your gratitude for two wonderful months' worth of coffee, sugar, beans, rice, and soup; the chance to take a day off and still be able to call Zoya; and a little money for emergencies. I will also write to Martin and Kate, asking for their input on a possible Arabella [phone] companion for [your daughter] Talia. I'll get back to you with their response the next time we visit.

I am pleased to report that I am coughing less; Mr. Trump hasn't tweeted anything today; and my chocolate supply will still fortify an army, and the expected ice and snow have not yet arrived.

Peace,
Annie

*****

Emails: January 16, 2018
Subject: Ahmed's case—the latest briefs

[Annie to Warren]

I know the briefs from both sides are now in. You might not have received the prosecution's papers yet. When you get them, I would really appreciate knowing where the prosecution is focusing its efforts and what we can do now to address their objections and thus minimize the possibility of another remand from the BIA. Specifically ...

I fear the prosecution will make a big deal about the Judge's pushing forward without DHS's ability to cross-examine or present their case well. I fear that could generate another remand.

I wonder if DHS has brought up any other new issues we weren't anticipating and how we minimize the possibility of remand because of them.

Hopefully, when the judge writes up her decision, she will have crossed all the "t"s and dotted all the "i"s. I think she will want to go out on a triumphant note and will take great care writing her decision this time. But Dang. Dumb stuff with dire consequences has happened. So we will need to be vigilant…and diplomatic…and get it right.

Ahmed looked discouraged today. The domestic situation is understandably a challenge. I am doing what I can to hook up emotional support for Zoya and Talia from the Arabella community.

[Warren to Annie]

Interestingly enough, I did get their submission today. However, rather than submitting any additional argument, they just submitted news articles about how a few Al-Shabaab militants surrendered to the Somali government and how the U.S. recently had an increased military presence in Somalia. I guess they're still arguing that it's safe to return there.

I share your concern about how the last proceeding was conducted, but there were no objections until the end, and additional testimony was not necessarily required. I think the judge—and appeals court—knows where all parties stand, and we have argued the case ad nauseam at this point. We can wait for the judge's decision and go from there. I will thoroughly review it to see if there are any issues, but as you said, I think the judge will be extra careful this time. I politely reminded her of this in court and in our brief, we submitted last. Everybody wants to avoid an appeal, but that may be unavoidable. However, we can ensure that any further appeal is limited to asylum law, not some strange procedural issue.

I'll be in touch with any decision, which should probably be coming in the next few weeks.

Ahmed

Annie shared with me the following email she received from Mr. Warren:

Email: January 26, 2018
Subject: Ahmed update

[Warren to Annie]

The Immigration Judge once again granted Ahmed "relief." I don't have the decision yet (this should come on Monday), but I'm sure it was Asylum for the third time (the other option would be relief under the Convention Against Torture). DHS has until 2/26 to appeal.

Once I get the decision, I'll make sure there were no [unanticipated] legal issues or conclusions reached and then call the head DHS attorney in the region and try to convince him not to appeal a third time. Fingers crossed, and I'll keep you updated.

I was surprised that I had been given asylum for the third time because I sensed that the judge had been put under tremendous pressure because of all the appeals. But Judge Alexander clearly demonstrated professionalism, compassion, and fairness toward me and my case. I felt it would be easy for her to consider: *Why, why do you care about this guy? You should just use your pen and book removal. That's it, you know, let him go.* But Ms. Helen would not think of that. She was consistent with what she believed and how she handled the case. She even mentioned to me after the last hearing that, unless the counselor presented unexpected evidence, she would keep granting me asylum!

Michael

Although the judge had granted Ahmed asylum for the third time, DHS announced it would appeal again. Appeal briefs were due by mid-May. This left us all waiting again for the briefs and then the subsequent decision by the board.

In her written decision for asylum, Judge Alexander repeated all the arguments that Warren had made in his brief. But in this third decision, she narrowed the case to asylum only, not addressing relief under "Withholding of Removal" because Ahmed had given sufficient proof he deserved asylum.

Withholding of removal would never be acceptable to Ahmed. A person being granted that cannot petition to bring family members to the United States and does not gain a path to permanent residence, let alone citizenship. This would amount to a bandage fix, a temporary thing, where they could send Ahmed back to Somalia at any time.

Likewise, for CAT, Judge Alexander had not addressed it previously because of her decision for asylum. However, she discussed the evidence for CAT to satisfy the BIA request. Most notably, she maintained that the Somali government has been actively fighting Al-Shabaab with the help of the international community. Thus, she negated one condition for relief under the CAT.

The judge concluded her written decision with two orders. She granted Ahmed asylum again and denied Ahmed relief under CAT.

18

Liberty

> An angel of the Lord appeared, and a light shone in the cell—tapping Peter's side, he said to him, "Get up! Rise quickly!" And the chains fell from his hands.
>
> —Acts 12:7

Ahmed

February 2, 2018—Arabella, Iowa

One of the deportation officers from ICE, an African American officer, came to me on a Friday. Together, we went to a meeting room. "We are going to release you. You have an address," he said. "Be quiet about this. None of us wants a disturbance."

"Yes, sir," I said. "Thank you, sir."

I went back to my cell, walking about a foot off the floor. *Is it true?* I couldn't believe it!

As soon as I had some free time, I phoned Warren and then Annie. Warren told me the earliest they would release me would be Monday, which he had arranged with ICE, and Annie told me she and Michael planned to pick me up then.

Annie seemed so very excited. "Michael and I are looking forward to your release. We will meet you at the jail. We will have everything ready for you when you come to our home."

I didn't know what to say. "Yes, I'll be ready," I said. "Thank you. See you on Monday. Thank you."

On Monday, right after lunch, there was a quarrel, shouting, and some pushing and shoving. The guards ordered a lockdown. They put all the inmates back in their cells until things became quiet, and then they conducted a strip-search of the inmates responsible. This was standard procedure.

Finally, as I was being led out into the reception area, my name was called out so everyone in my cell block could hear. After eighteen months, hearing my name was like music to my ears. I received a standing ovation from the inmates and some guards. I had their respect. They were all happy for me. I was getting out after so many months of jail. Then the camera took one more picture, which was one more indication that I was leaving MCC.

As I came down the elevator toward the exit of the jail, my thinking was jumbled. I was not organized. I had wanted to dress up, but no, I was wearing my tracksuit. This was a big moment. I'd be meeting Michael for the first time. But overall, I felt wonderful. I can't really describe it.

Michael was inside the waiting area, and Annie was just outside in a glassed-in room where the exit was. They both had waited for several hours until late afternoon because of the disturbance upstairs.

When Michael saw me, he called my name, got up, and shook my hand. I was struggling with two plastic bags of clothing and other articles they had kept from me while in jail. We just stood there smiling at each other. Then Michael gave me a quick hug and opened the door to where Annie was standing. I gave her a big hug. She kissed me on my cheek, and the three of us could not decide whether to cry or laugh. It had been a long, long time waiting—626 days since I entered that jail.

Outside, the air was chilly. It was getting dark, and it was snowing. Before I got inside the car, I grabbed some snow. I wanted to touch it. I wanted to feel it. Driving on the way to my new home was like, you know, my mind was absent. *Was this really happening?*

Coming to my new home and being welcomed to a house with a bedroom and bathroom just for me was more than I could have hoped for. I took a shower, slept in an actual bed, and felt like a human again. And when Annie came to wake me up, it was like I had only closed my eyes. I was reminded that I was truly out of jail. What a good feeling, a wonderful memory I would never forget.

Many mornings after they released me, when I woke up in my new surroundings, my first thought was that I was still dreaming. I only needed to close my eyes, open them again, and see myself back in MCC. The experience of jail was so fresh in my mind.

*****

Before February was over, Mr. Warren received a notice that the DHS lawyer would appeal again. I thought we had answered all their questions and there would no longer be any disagreements. *Three times being granted asylum was enough*! They must be arguing over the same stuff.

I knew in my heart that I wasn't truly on solid ground after all, not on the sure path toward asylum. And this time, because I was no longer detained in jail, it would take twice as long, maybe a year, for the BIA to come back with a decision. Annie had sent me some information about Canada last summer, and Michael had loaned me his laptop. Now I had the chance to look at going to Canada as one of my options. Here is some info I found on the Canadian government website (Immigration 2018):

Regarding Refugee Resettlement in Canada:

- The United Nations Refugee Agency (UNHCR) identifies refugees for resettlement. A person cannot apply directly to Canada for resettlement.

- Private sponsors across the country also help resettle refugees to Canada. Some do this on an ongoing basis. They have signed sponsorship agreements with the Government of Canada to help support refugees.
- Resettlement Times are based on how long it took to process 80% of the applications in the past.

Government of Canada Application Processing Times:

- Refugee, Government-assisted
  - from Somalia   22 months
  - from South Africa   22 months
- Refugee, Private-sponsored
  - from Somalia   52 months
  - from South Africa   70 months
- Convention Refugee
  - already in Canada   22 months for a final decision

I learned from the same website that "Convention Refugee—already in Canada" was a person who had a well-founded fear of persecution according to the *convention* that was law in Canada. And the convention, based on the same *five protected grounds* of persecution, was like what they used in the US. So possible asylum in Canada was an option I considered if I lost my case in the US.

19

Our Home Is Your Home

> Love is that condition in which the happiness of
> another person is essential to your own.
>
> —Robert A. Heinlein, *Stranger in a Strange Land*

Annie

Michael and I could not contain our joy! After almost two years, Ahmed would be released from detention, from jail. I knew this was a precious moment for him and the beginning of a huge transformation to his life. And I was excited for Michael. He would finally meet him.

Ahmed would live with us for as long as it took for him to get asylum and beyond, whatever he needed. He would come home with us.

On a frosty February afternoon, the air was crisp outside but stale and unfriendly in the waiting room. We had waited several hours without an answer to my question to the guards at reception. "Any news when he might be released?"

One of the guards called the desk upstairs. "No one knows when he will be released," he said.

I asked again, late in the afternoon. "When will Ahmed be released." There was a new guard after the shift change at 3:00 p.m.

"Doesn't look like it will happen today," he said. I waited for him to add, "Have a nice day."

"I'll continue to wait," I said.

Michael said he would remain inside so he could hear any announcements from the guard. Meanwhile, I waited in the glass-enclosed entrance. I could keep and use my phone there. I wanted to be available for possible calls from Warren.

It was getting dark outside, after five o'clock, when I looked up from my phone, and there he was. I saw Ahmed standing before Michael. He was carrying two big plastic bags stuffed with his clothes and personal things. I waited.

And I watched Ahmed smile at Michael. His smile was charming and contagious, with a bit of mirth thrown in. Although Ahmed had asked me about my husband during our many visits, it was their first meeting. He was certainly glad to meet Michael, but much more than that, Ahmed looked full of joy—to be out of confinement and more than ready to start living again.

It had turned cloudy, with light snow falling, and dark, except for streetlights and headlights reflecting the snow. Ahmed took the front seat next to Michael and was sitting silently, looking at everything he could see outside the window. I could tell he was overflowing with emotion and wonder.

"Look up there. See that small window?" he said. "That must be the window I looked out all those days. And there is that tall building, the only thing I could see."

*****

After Ahmed got settled into his new room, we talked for a little while. It was getting close to suppertime, and he wanted to cook a meal for us. He had been cooking at the jail and was quite good at it, so he wanted to treat us, and he was going to cook for us—to cook for us forever—to say thank you. He made a nice red sauce to go with the halal meat I had on hand for him, along with some onions, green peppers, and rice. On the stove, it looked like a lovely meal. "I'm going to cook for you every day," Ahmed said. "This is something I can do for you."

I smiled. "Well, Michael and I don't eat at the same time or eat the same thing. We're on different schedules and expected you to be the same way."

"Okay, but you must tell me what other things I can do for you."

"Okay," I said. "You're going to be off doing your own things and eating foods that are very comfortable for you from your heritage. And besides, it's about time you had much more control over your life." And I showed him where the pantry was. "We're going to go shopping. Here's an extra space here. This is going to be where your choices go for your food. You can eat when you want. You can eat what you want. It's up to you if you want to cook or not. The only thing I'm pretty big on is to open the door if you're cooking garlic. Otherwise, you're free. Please do what you wish and have at it."

That night, Ahmed had already cooked for us. It looked well prepared and tasted good. But even though we told him not to make it very spicy, it made me choke. Here was a man who could eat a whole jalapeno and not even blink. Ultimately, I was glad for my little dissertation that he should cook only for himself, and Michael was indebted to me for this arrangement.

That evening, Ahmed went to bed at about eight o'clock, and he seemed so exhausted that he must have just fallen into bed. And we checked on him the next morning because we had not heard a peep and wanted to ensure he was okay. I knocked on the door. "How are you doing in there?"

"Did I leave a light on? Did I leave my stuff in the hall?" he asked.

"No. Just checking. It looks like it will be a beautiful, sunny day."

"Oh," and he started laughing. "I thought it was still night, that I was asleep only a few minutes." He was that zonked out, and the time flew by. In the silence, his body knew what to do: just sleep.

We went shopping then. ALDI Grocery became his favorite store because it was small and inexpensive. Ahmed wanted to spend less money. He could make selections rather readily instead of being overwhelmed by all the choices at a Hy-Vee or Walmart. So off to ALDI we would go, and he quickly spotted the things he wanted and got what he needed. He would pick up rice or macaroni and tuna in a can, beans, potatoes, hot peppers, onion, tomatoes, garlic bread, sandwich bread, and peanut butter.

Ahmed found his very best favorite food of all time when I bought him string cheese. He loved that string cheese. He was so used to everything being rationed. He rationed everything, even when he got out of jail at our home. And so he had only one piece of string cheese, then went to bed and told us the next day that he wanted more of that string cheese so badly, he got up in the middle of the night and had a second piece, like that was the most fantastic food and freedom he ever had.

And we were just delighted again that this was heaven for him. He had his own bathroom, and he could shower whenever he wanted to in the way he needed to because of the practices of Islam. Ahmed was a religious man who read the Koran in Arabic and prayed many times each day whenever he had the chance. As soon as we could, we took him to a local mosque where he could pray with other Muslims and meet the Imam.

*****

Ahmed had a couple of things that were high on his agenda: obtaining a phone and getting reconnected with his family. Michael was ready to make this happen. The two of them went off to Walmart to find a phone he could afford and easily FaceTime with his family on. If you want to know how to make phone calls internationally and cheaply, you want to talk to an immigrant, a refugee.

And I thought, *Oh boy, he would want to call them right away.* Nope. When he was going to be seen by his family, he would look his very best.

When Ahmed was still in jail, I asked Warren to please request that the family email some pictures of themselves for their father. I put those photos into a collective portrait and gave it to Ahmed on one of my visits. He had not seen them in several years, but when those pictures came, he cried, and he commented on how beautifully dressed they were.

I had a three-sided folding mirror for cutting one's hair. It came with an instructional video on a CD, and it was intended for African American men. It included different styles, so I gave him the complete kit: clippers, the video, and the mirror. And Ahmed came out after some time in his bathroom with his hair cut just beautifully. And then he wanted to get dressed up in his best shirt. He confided to me, "I will look fantastic when they see me on the phone."

Ahmed knew the best time to call his family, when they were all together. Zoya was walking the kids to school one day. And suddenly, up on her cell phone came some request that Ahmed would like to be one of her contacts. And she started screaming, "Ahmed is a contact! Ahmed is on my phone!"

She tapped yes to that request. And then her phone rang, and it was Ahmed and the screaming that went on! He was in his bedroom with the door shut, and I was in the living room on the far side of the house. I could hear the screams of joy because there was their father, there was Zoya's husband, and they could see him. And they were full of questions. "Where are you? What happened? Why can we see you? We are so worried about you."

"I'm at Annie and Michael's house," he said. "They let me out of jail."

More screams!

Ahmed had made a visual connection with his family, the barriers were coming down, and he was reunited with them after such a long time. And they could talk as long as they wanted and see each other's smiles.

*****

One of the first things I did was to line up Ahmed for a physical. I took him to a place called Arabella Community Health. This was a neighborhood health care clinic with an open-door policy that served people even though they might have no insurance and/or little income. I explained his situation, so they placed him on the very bottom of the sliding scale. They charged him only thirty-five dollars for the physical. "That is quite a lot to pay," he said.

"Not for someone with income, even if they have insurance," I said. "It can get quite expensive."

Ahmed was impressed and touched by the attention and kindness he received. The medical staff treated him respectfully, asked him questions, and listened carefully, a big step up when compared to what he experienced in jail.

Michael had a two-year-old laptop that he rarely used. He loaned it to Ahmed and later gave it to him. Ahmed took to that like a duck to water. He got on the Internet and connected with Somali organizations, started learning Microsoft applications, researched immigration questions, and looked for ways to connect with programs for refugees. It was just amazing to him the freedom he enjoyed—his phone, laptop, quiet room, and good food.

Ahmed was not big on taking walks, even in our neighborhood. I thought he would like to get out and walk the beautiful trails, but he was too afraid that ICE would come and get him. He lived in the world of refugees, which is very scary.

"ICE can pick you up for no reason, and you can wind up back in jail until they figure out what's going on," he told me. So even though I went with him when we went out together, in those first weeks, he stayed close to me and made sure we didn't go far. He was not even excited about sitting in a rocker on our front porch. He would rather people didn't know where he was and ICE couldn't find him.

*****

Ahmed had been attending jail school to get his GED. There was a volunteer who would come in, and she was helping four inmates with the English part of the GED program. Ahmed got very far in his studies and got up to where he could take a test for English, but he seemed very shy about taking tests and never quite got to where he said he would take them. That was part of it. Also, when he was trying to study in jail, it was so stressful there, he found it tough to focus. I thought he would like to take the English and math test now that he was out of jail. He tried, but he always seemed to progress slowly even though he talked very confidently. There was a resistance that he could not do this anymore. I felt he was mentally worn out, tired of concentrating.

When we had talked about coding school when he got out of jail, he was sure he would have no problems taking that on. If you had the aptitude, you could go into coding school without a degree, just with who you were. And if you passed the beginning test, you could get into a program, go to coding boot camp, and come out and have a great job.

But I needed to check with Warren, see if he could make this happen.

> Emails: February 12, 2018
> Subject: Ahmed and meeting with ICE
>
> [Annie to Warren]
>
> Ahmed hopes to attend a 13-week programming school in Provo, Utah, the one starting on March 19. He checked with ISAP [Intensive Supervision Appearance Program] this morning, and they would need fifteen days' notice along with his address at the school, but they had no problem with him traveling there and would pick up the task of monitoring him there.
>
> But Ahmed would also need to obtain a travel document from ICE and check in with them once a month, starting March 7.
>
> At the scheduled meeting with his deportation officer on March 7, he could ask for a travel document, but that would be too late to notify

ISAP and too close to the time he would be traveling to be sure to get an airline ticket.

So, he is asking if you could set up a meeting with his deportation officer to obtain permission to travel and acquire the necessary travel documents. It would be greatly appreciated if this could be done this week or next week!

[Warren to Annie]

I will certainly ask for this permission this week and will be in touch with the response. We can also file for Ahmed's work permit now, as I've clarified a few things. Please let us know when he can come in to sign the application. I'll also need two passport-size photos of him.

Email: February 13, 2018
Subject: Ahmed and meeting with ICE

[Warren to Annie]

We're good to go on the schooling! Just check in with [the ICE office in] Arabella on 3/7 and not again until he returns to Arabella on 7/11.

I sent him a book on coding when he was in jail, and it didn't go anywhere then. And despite his claims when he came out that "I can do anything, Annie, anything I put my mind to—I am not a quitter—I know I can do this coding school," it became insurmountable to him.

The most promising coding school had an initial exam. They said they would look at admission if he could get through that exam. So Ahmed started on that test but could not get past the first question, even with Michael helping him. It was just beyond him. And it was so hard for Ahmed to admit this—the can-do guy, for the first time, could not do it. We quietly dropped it and looked at other possibilities.

20

Mom and Dad

Family is not an important thing, it's everything.

—Michael J. Fox

Annie

Emails: February 28, 2018
Subject: DHS Appeal

[Warren to Annie]

 As expected, we received the DHS notice of appeal this week. They're arguing everything as expected. They did acknowledge that it's a non-detained case, so everything slows down, and the appeals process could take a year or so until the final resolution. We'll be in touch, but this will give [Ahmed] plenty of time to complete school!

[Annie to Warren]

Yes, the focus of the appeal is as expected (unfortunately). I have two questions about processing time:

The last time we spoke, you said that the appeals process could go extra fast because this is the 3rd time around in the BIA, or it could slow down because Ahmed is out of jail. You didn't know which way it would go.

Is it for sure that the process will slow down to a year?

The thirteen-week time frame for the coding course Ahmed was going to take is no longer an issue. If Ahmed wanted, is there a way to request the court expedite the case because this is the third appeal?

Thanks for the information that will help him decide on the next steps.

[Warren to Annie]

Yes, I believe this could easily take six months to a year, even though it's round three. Everything slows down when someone is not in custody. There's nothing to do to speed it up since it's not our appeal. We will have to wait this out and respond to the government when the time comes.

On March 19, Ahmed went in for EAD Biometrics, a medical checkup the government needed as part of his work permit application. Since it looked like he would wait a long time for the BIA's decision, it would be good for him to get a job and make some money to send to his family.

> Emails: April 9–10, 2018
> Subject: Briefs due—Ahmed
>
> [Annie to Warren]
>
> We are all pleased that the due date for submitting briefs has been set—for April 26. We're on track to move forward! I've got two quick questions:
>
> Will you see the other side's brief before you need to write up Ahmed's? I think you mentioned we would have an advantage this time.
>
> Your fee is likely due now as you will be working on the brief. Just checking: was it $2,000? We can get that to you as soon as we verify the amount.
>
> Ahmed is studying hard on his GED, getting to know the town, and making friends. He's looking forward to the work permit, which will allow him to take the driving test and GED exams.
>
> Things at his home have *vastly* improved since you got him released. He connects (on video) with family every day. They plan and laugh, and problem-solve together. You put the pieces back together. And they are doing very well.
>
> [Warren to Annie]

I just received that briefing schedule, too, and was a bit surprised that they are still treating him as detained—hence the relatively quick turnaround time. This also does not give us the luxury of seeing DHS's argument before ours is submitted since we have to submit simultaneous briefs. I'm also out of town for some time this month, so if Ahmed agrees, now that he's out of detention, I was thinking about asking for a three-week extension to file our brief. $2000 should cover the fees as well.

I'm glad to hear about Ahmed acclimating. Hopefully, his work permit will come soon. The one concern may be his lack of passport/government ID from Somalia. Can you please ask him if he had a real Somali passport when he came or a fake one?

I'm also pleased to hear that he can speak with his family. That should hopefully boost everyone's spirits. Hopefully, we can finish this successfully this time around and once and for all!

[Annie to Warren]

We will talk to Ahmed in the morning about the possible three-week extension and the ID issue. But before we do, Michael and I are panicking a bit here, wondering how the passport/Government ID relates to the ability to work. How is the ID part of getting authorization to work? Significant funding from his South African benefactor for his family is due to end in August.

[Warren to Annie]

It's a requirement that they've gotten much more strict about enforcing recently (honestly, we found out the hard way about this for the first time yesterday). To play it safe, it would be best if Ahmed reached out to the Somali embassy in DC to see if they can get him anything from there proving his nationality/citizenship.

[Annie to Warren]

There is confusion here… For my part, you seem to be saying that administrators processing the work permit will require proof of national citizenship. Yet I thought Asylees are a different case, that they are not expected to have a passport because of their dramatic circumstances, even when applying for a Green Card.

Ahmed knows that the U.S. Somali Embassy will not issue passports to anyone with a pending case. He also believes that if the U.S. Somali embassy could supply a passport, it would be used against him if his case was overturned. ICE could use that passport to ship him out on the first flight. So, getting one would be dangerous.

A three-week extension is acceptable. We are wondering if the process itself will add additional time.

Let's hope we can clear up some confusion in a conversation tomorrow.

Thanks for helping move the case forward.

[Warren to Annie]

All work permits require a government form of ID regardless of the underlying application they are based on. We just submit a copy of the biographic page or ID, not the original. They will probably deny the application if we don't provide it. They haven't asked yet, but I anticipate they will need it based on other recent cases.

The three-week delay shouldn't affect anything beyond the three weeks. The processing times will be the same.

*****

Ahmed started doing more hands-on stuff, physical stuff. We had wanted to finish part of our garage, so Ahmed helped Michael with the wallboard, putting that up, and I did the taping. Once that was dry, I taught Ahmed how to paint. He was excited, so I gave him a roller and a bucket of paint, and we started painting together. On his side, he just went at it as fast as he could, slapping it on in one thick layer, and he was very proud of himself. We waited for it to dry.

After that, I showed him how I was doing it a different way and slower, and you could see that where he had painted, it didn't have much coverage, and mine covered everything. So I taught him how to paint in the W method, and he was eager to learn. He was tall enough to do the ceiling without standing on a ladder. That helped us out a great deal. He had noticed how we organized everything, which is typical of me. Every piece of equipment had a place to go, and he helped us put the place back together again.

Michael came up with a great idea. He was volunteering for Habitat ReStore, so he went to talk to them about Ahmed, who wanted to work but could not. He had no worker's permit. So Michael asked them if Ahmed could volunteer for them.

The store manager said they'd be glad to have him. He put him to work, accepting drop-off donations, stocking shelves, and sorting things, which was a perfect match for him. He fit right in. He was such a hard worker. He cleaned, dusted, organized, and had great ideas for where things should be. They would ask him to do a task, and he would do it. And he started at just a few hours a week and then just about every other day or every day. He enjoyed it so much. Michael paid Ahmed ten dollars an hour to give him his spending money to dignify the situation, which became a way to support Habitat further. Ahmed made friends there and so got connected to the broader community.

*****

When Ahmed got out of jail and we gave him great, big hugs, nobody could control that expression, that outpouring of emotion. But there was still a sense that I wanted to respect any cultural norms that had restrictions or some divides around gender and who could hug whom and who could not. It had been obvious in the jail what the rules were. You could not shake hands; you couldn't touch; there would be no other physical contact; you could only talk. That was a jail where they wanted nothing going back and forth between people. Expressions of affection were limited to facial expressions and verbal interactions.

I understood Ahmed. I knew him, his story, and he knew me, and we cared a great deal for each other, but I needed to be very careful around this. I was so unlike our friend Lucy, who came through the door, grabbed Ahmed, and gave him the biggest hug in the world. She was like, *I don't care if you like this. You are getting a giant hug.*

I was in a much more complicated situation: he was living with us. And so what eventually rolled out was when we welcomed him into our home, we said, "You are family. You are part of our family now. Here is your room, and we will care for each other as a family." And this helped the relationship and the understanding of how I related to Ahmed in terms of touch.

Soon afterward, he started calling me "Mom" and Michael "Dad." And because of that, I didn't feel there were the customary restrictions around giving hugs, and neither did Ahmed. Yeah, giving hugs or high fives or whatever you might do in a family was perfectly okay. I could very dearly give him a hug and, you know, maybe a peck on the cheek and say, "I really care about you, son," and he could say, "I love you, Mom." And it cleared everything up very neatly.

We welcomed him to the family, and what was unclear became clear. Expressions of affection broke through immediately. This extended further: his family became our family, and our family became wider than ever.

*****

On May 15, the employment authorization application (EAD) came back denied. One of Warren's legal assistants had inadvertently checked the wrong box that did not apply to Ahmed. Warren tried to contact someone who could clear this up—check a different box on the form—but there was no one to talk to, no process in place to do this. So the entire form had to be resubmitted. It was like going to the back of the line and starting over.

On May 17, the appeal briefs were submitted to the BIA by Counselor Taylor of the DHS and Attorney Jackson. We read the DHS brief together with Ahmed. "That's not true!" Ahmed said. "And that's not true, and that's not true."

I sensed that Ahmed was offended. The counselor's brief was disturbing! Ms. Taylor twisted what Ahmed had testified this way and that. She was trying everything to discredit him, and there were many baseless allegations.

Ahmed experienced our startled reactions but also wanted to see what his attorney had to say.

    Emails: May 24, 2018
    Subject: DHS

    [Ahmed to Warren]

Mr. Warren,

I hope you are well. Is it acceptable practice for the DHS to lie? Attached are alarming lies and accusations which I have found in DHS's latest brief. This is bothering me.

Attachment: DHS-inconsistent.docx

[Warren to Ahmed]

Thank you, Ahmed. While they are free to set forth their arguments and interpretations of the law (which the BIA should see through), we will draw attention to the factual inaccuracies and mischaracterizations in a reply brief.

Unfortunately, I have experienced numerous cases where the government attorney assigned to your case has exhibited the most unscrupulous behavior of them all in Arabella.

The following day, Ahmed shared Warren's email with me. I could not let this go without sounding off to Warren, and Michael chimed in as well:

Emails: May 25, 2018
Subject: Government Attorney's Behavior

[Annie to Warren; cc: Michael]

The behavior of this government attorney sullies the reputation of American justice. It makes me deeply ashamed of my country. And angry. She cares not a whit about the suffering her unscrupulous behavior causes or the lives she puts at risk. When the "Me Too" moment comes for her, the question will be, "What did the community do to stop her?" I wish there were more to be done besides putting such destructive behavior on the record.

[Michael to Warren; cc: Annie]

I am happy you will submit a reply brief; *it is well worth an additional fee*. To me, it looks like the government attorney is now resting their arguments on fabricated "quotes" and further twisting their arguments in an effort to obfuscate the truth.

[Warren to Annie and Michael]

All,

I have attached what I express-mailed to the BIA yesterday. I pointed out the most glaring lies or misrepresentations from DHS's most recent appeal brief.

Attachments: Motion to accept…and Reply Brief to 3rd DHS Appeal

21

Intensive Supervision

Happy is the man who has broken the chains which hurt the mind, and has given up worrying once and for all.

—Ovid

Michael

When the DHS deputy chief counselor, after many petitions by Attorney Jackson, finally granted Ahmed release from jail, he was released "on his own recognizance" and monitored by a third party under the "Intensive Supervision and Appearance Program" (ISAP). A bracelet equipped with a GPS and radio transmitter was fastened securely to his ankle. The company monitoring him would know immediately if he left the Arabella metro.

In addition, he had a stay-at-home day every Tuesday, weekly visits to the ISAP contractor, and periodic visits to the offices of ICE. Annie and I filled out a form and provided two more names, Lucy and Elanor, with all our phone numbers listed. If ISAP needed to contact Ahmed and he wasn't answering, they would call each person on the list in an attempt to get hold of him.

The GPS ankle bracelet, which continually chafed at Ahmed's ankle, would require nightly charging of its battery. On the many occasions that the unit had problems (it would stop transmitting)

Ahmed would need to go to the ISAP offices the next morning to get the battery or unit replaced.

For all these trips, I would be the driver. This gave me lots of time to get to know Ahmed better and learn more about his situation. "Were there many immigrants in jail while you were there?" I asked.

"No," Ahmed said, "only a handful of immigration cases, only five of us."

"And did you get to know most of them?"

"Yes. We were really connected. We would discuss our cases, the way forward, what to expect, and if there were any updates. If someone went to the courts, afterward, we would sit with him and ask him what the most difficult questions were, and how did he answer them. We were really helping one another. Yeah, so we knew one another quite well."

"What countries were the five of you from?"

"One was from Liberia. Kazeem was from South Sudan and had already served for ten years in jail. He was transferred from another jail, and he was divorced. Others were Kumar, a Somalian, one guy from Eritrea, and me."

"It sounds like the one from South Sudan had committed a crime, and that's why he was there?"

"Yeah. Well, once he has served his sentence, the court will hand him over to ICE, and then they will deport him because he isn't an American citizen."

"And the other Somalis," I asked, "were they like you as far as just waiting a long time for court proceedings?"

"Unfortunately, the Somalis were all deported, so I am the only one left," Ahmed said. "And I was the only one released from jail—in almost two years!"

"Did they have lawyers?" I was trying to understand. "Did they just not have a very good case? Do you know why they were refused asylum?"

"They had lawyers, but they all lost their cases, and some of them lost their second appeal. And as a result, they were all deported."

We rode on in silence for a while, attending to our own thoughts.

"Well, we've arrived," I said. "Let's hope they fix your ankle tracker once and for all so we don't have to keep making these trips downtown."

22

Pursuit of Happiness

> When I went to school, they asked me what I wanted to be when I grew up. I wrote down 'happy.'
>
> —attributed to John Lennon

Lucy

When Ahmed finally got out of jail, I was so excited to meet him, but I didn't want to overwhelm him either, and I know he was overwhelmed just by getting out of prison, being in society again, and staying at Annie and Michael's. I took him shopping for winter clothes. He had no boots; he had no heavy pants. There was no heavy coat on him. And you know, I'm a mom; what do moms do best? We shop, and we get our kids what they need.

I went to Annie and Michael's house and was excited to meet him in person. And I remember hugging him, and it's very odd to hug, supposedly, a stranger, but for some reason, he was not a stranger. Even though we had never spoken, the first thing he said was, "Thank you so much for coming to support me. Thank you so much for coming to the hearing." Gratitude poured out of him, and oh, his eyes were so bright, his smile was so big, and he was just nothing but gratitude.

"Well, we are going to do some shopping. We're going to get you some things you need," I said.

It was a nice little break for Annie and Michael because Ahmed had been in their house for a while. It wasn't a big deal, except it was so cold outside. We went to the local Target down the road. We walked into the store, and he just stopped at the door. He was looking around and being overwhelmed by it, just utterly overwhelmed. And of course, I was like, *Okay, where's the men's department?* I didn't even think about it twice.

As we walked through the store, his jaw dropped, and he followed me all around. He had no idea where we were going or what we were doing. I started getting frustrated because they were already into spring and summer clothing. And here it was February, and I had a tough time finding clothes for him and boots for him because the season was ending.

As we shopped through the store, I was like a crazy woman, going from department to department and trying to find things. Ahmed just followed me around and repeatedly said, "This is plenty. This is plenty."

"Okay, here's a pair of pants," I said. "Let's figure out your size and how big you are."

"Oh, any of them will do. Any of them will do," he said. He had no sense of what size pants he wore those days.

It was a kind of clash of cultures because he was amazed that anyone could walk through a store and pull anything off the shelf and, you know, pull anything off the rack and say, "Okay, I'm going to buy this. I'm going to buy that," without concern for a price. But more than that, he was surprised that a shopper would not have to ask for something from someone behind a counter, or they would be seen as stealing.

We found a pair of heavy pants that seemed to fit, and then he sat and tried on some winter boots. He got a heavy coat, a vest, and a stocking cap to bundle up for winter, a season they did not have in Somalia, not like we do here.

And he was so grateful. Whichever selection it was, "This will be fine," he said. "Oh, that'll be fine."

It was such a joy for me. It was such an immense delight to give so directly to someone who had suffered so much. I mean, I would have bought him the whole damn store, but he kept saying, "No, this is enough. This is enough."

My family is not superwealthy, but we have far more than we need or more than Ahmed has ever experienced, and I wanted him to be safe and warm and know that we had his back and that he deserved to live with human dignity. He was out in this crazy American culture he wasn't used to, and in some ways, I felt bad that I was more focused on finding him what he needed than recognizing how overwhelming the experience must have been for him.

*****

It was the beginning of spring now, and I knew Ahmed had been spending a lot of time over at Annie and Michael's, and they were trying to find things to keep him busy. And I thought they kept him in jail for so long that it would be fun to do outdoor stuff with him, so I asked if he would like to help me plant flowers in my garden. I bought a bunch of mums and other flowers for my front yard.

But I had to go to work that day, so I got everything ready for when he came over, and we could plant the flowers together. So I set everything out early before I went to work and had all the tools out and put each pot near where I wanted it, and I dropped bags of potting soil here and there.

Ahmed was very excited and very grateful. "I'll help you do anything," he said. "I'll help you do anything. Whatever I can help with is fine."

When I pulled into the driveway, I saw it was already done. The flowers were all planted, perfectly done. And here I had thought I was going to be spending my evening in the dirt and trying to get this task done after a long day of work. And Ahmed was sitting on my front lawn, leaning back on his hands, enjoying the sunshine.

He had planted all my flowers exactly where I wanted them. I don't know how he did it. He must have worked like a fiend, and I had not expected him to. I intended it to be something we would do together. And he was, again, smiling so big. It was beautiful to see him just savoring nature outside and under a tree. I got out of my car and was like, "Oh my gosh, how did you do this so fast?"

"This is heaven to be outside," he said.

The flowers looked beautiful! He had done a fantastic job. "Here, let me pay you," I said.

But he would not let me. At my insistence, he relented and cheerfully said, "It will be an anonymous donation to my fund." That made us both laugh.

This gift surprised me, and I learned a little more about him. One thing Ahmed so enjoyed was a surprise, especially when he did the surprising.

*****

Ahmed stayed for dinner that night, which was wonderful to share a meal with him and have him meet my family. My four kids happened to be at home that evening. It excited them to meet him. But *excitement* would not be the best word for Layla, my oldest—more like *suspicion*. Layla came from Ethiopia as a teenager, but at that time, she was about twenty-three. Layla spoke English quite well but also Amharic, her native tongue. That was one of many languages Ahmed could speak because of his Ethiopian wife. It was fascinating when the two of them met. My daughter, having lived in Ethiopia until she was fifteen, had an impression of Somalis and what they might be like and, you know, her cultural baggage.

But they sat and started talking in Amharic, and I had no idea what they were saying. And within like twenty minutes, they were laughing. It wasn't even twenty; I'd say in ten minutes, they were laughing and joking. "What was that conversation about?" I asked Layla later.

"Oh, things about Africa and cultural things here that drive both of us crazy."

Even though I had told Ahmed's story to Layla, she had been wary because he was a Somali man, and she had been conditioned to be cautious of them. And I think for both of them, it was so comforting to speak their common African language again that he won her over so fast.

Over the summer, we had several random dinners at our house, just backyard barbecues and things like that, that Ahmed would attend with Annie and Michael. At all of them, he was always so helpful—so smiley, so appreciative, so inspiring, so fun to be with, and so engaging. "Let me help," Ahmed would say. "Let me help. Let me help." It was like he was part of the family. But secretly, I wished my kids would say those words more often.

*****

Sometime later that spring, my youngest daughter Lily and I made a day trip to Omaha's zoo with him. There's a big indoor jungle at the zoo, and it's very open, where birds fly around. There are tropical trees, you hear waterfalls, and it's humid, just like a jungle.

And yet it was hard for Ahmed to look at the animals, even in that ample space. Although it was laid out beautifully, the animals had to be behind an enclosure. He was choking up at seeing them being kept in a cage. He said it reminded him of his experience of how he was treated in the county jail. It must have been still fresh in his mind, so I wonder if the zoo was an overall happy experience for him. However, we got some magnificent pictures.

Still, he was amazed and delighted and noticed everything. He commented on the relatively free birds and monkeys, especially the animals from different parts of Africa. Exploring that world with him and my daughter Lily was fun.

*****

That summer, Ahmed invited us to what I would call an African picnic. I don't know if it was mainly a Somali celebration or if other ethnic groups were represented. There were lots of people dressed in colorful African attire. It was like walking a bit into his world. He had done the culture shock walking into ours. I felt like a fish out of water at this picnic, where almost everybody around me was from various parts of Africa and speaking different languages. But Ahmed had found a community. They had introduced him to some people who had immigrated, which was so good for him. I did not know if they all went through what he did.

I was watching his actions and reactions at that picnic. Most of all, he was concerned about us. "Do you have everything you need?" Ahmed asked. "Do you want more food?" and "Oh, let me get you this. Let me get you that." He was so, so concerned.

How wonderful I felt that he invited us into that community. He did not have to do that. And he wanted us to be a part of that world too, and that was so nice. I watched him interact with people with such joy and intensity. Everyone he talked to, he looked in the eye and was fully present with them. Anyone he spoke to, he smiled, and they smiled. And he found enjoyment in everybody and everything and was so gracious and connected with people so well. It was just fun to watch him be free in his world.

*****

One evening, after Ahmed had dinner with us, he and I discussed what I would call our Muslim-Christian dynamic. Ahmed and I agreed we were on the same spiritual wavelength. There was something more significant than all of us, connecting all of us. And even though he is a Muslim and I am a Christian, there was no differentiation between us in how we saw each other as somehow connected to that divine power.

I experienced that his faith was strong. It was inspiring. It reaffirmed for me the Islam divinity I have seen in many Muslims. I got a sense that Ahmed lived that faith and practiced that faith and fully exhibited the love that so many people refuse to see in the Islam faith.

Sadly, Islam carries such a negative connotation for so many non-Muslims in America. If they met Ahmed and saw this man exemplifying what it means to be a Muslim, I think many would become attracted to the Islamic faith.

There are so many things in various religions that are human constructs and expressions, but Ahmed and I agreed on what matters. We both have this sense of being children of God together in this world, and I love that we both could so freely acknowledge that.

23

When Two Elephants Fight

When two elephants fight, it is the grass that suffers.

—East African proverb

Michael

On May 16, 2018, DHS filed a "Brief on Appeal" with the BIA. The DHS counselor presented multiple issues that claimed the immigration judge made an error. Ms. Taylor maintained Ahmed did not meet the definition of a refugee because (1) the men giving the threats were not identified (they said nothing about who they were, and the letter did not identify them; the black flag symbol was not acceptable as a symbol of Al-Shabaab), (2) the two threats were vague ("face the consequences" and "he knows what to do"), and (3) the evidence did not show Ahmed's fear of persecution is based on one of the protected grounds (rather, the harm he fears is on account of the civil unrest, which affects everyone in Somalia).

Ms. Taylor claimed Ahmed was not a credible witness because he was inconsistent in his testimony, evasive during questioning, and contradicted himself multiple times. And there was no clear evidence to support his testimony. Lastly, Ms. Taylor insisted that the evidence failed to show that the government of Somalia is unable or unwilling to protect Ahmed from those seeking to do him harm.

After that, she spent seven pages of her brief trying to pick apart Ahmed's testimony to discredit him. To me, these arguments bordered on the ridiculous. Here are examples of issues with Ahmed's statements Ms. Taylor was raising, followed by my interpretations:

First, did they hand him the threat letter or drop it at his feet? To a Somali with English as a second language, it means the same thing: they used their hands to drop it at his feet.

Second, he said the masked men *came in* with papers and threw them on the ground, and at other times, he testified he was outside the hospital. Again, this is picking apart his English. Would he say ground if it were not outside?

Third, the number of other applicants, besides Ahmed, who also received a letter varied in his testimony—three men inside, three others outside with him, seven in total. Sometimes he said four but was including himself in those outside. Being badgered with questions and being told, "You said this" and "You said that" would confuse anyone, especially if your first language was not English.

Fourth, Ahmed had no conversations with "the masked men," nor did they attach any meaning to the two alleged threats, so the threats were vague. You must leave the country or "face the consequences" was not ambiguous in the least to Ahmed. The *modus operandi* of Al-Shabaab was to kill their enemies, not have a meeting to discuss things.

Fifth, Ahmed was evasive. If Ahmed did not mention everything the counselor wanted, did she give him questions to let him know that? Ms. Taylor found many things that Ahmed "failed to mention" that he had testified to before.

And last, the dialog between his sister and the masked men varied. At one point, Ahmed testified she said one thing, and at another, he testified she said something different. This could easily be two statements from the same conversation. Again, the counselor's reliance on proper English grammar and usage was in question.

DHS's last arguments showed me that although they viewed the same evidence and heard the same testimony as the immigration judge and Ahmed's attorney, the DHS counselor was quite emphatic in her conclusions that the judge had erred in her findings and consequent decision. It appeared to me that Counselor Taylor had discussed this case within the department, and she was not acting alone. Darcy Taylor signed every brief as assistant chief counsel. Directly under her signature were listed the names of her boss, the deputy chief counsel, and the top person in charge of the region, the chief counsel for US DHS-ICE.

Ms. Taylor argued against every issue connected with the question of Ahmed's asylum. She maintained the "mere threats" were vague, unfulfilled, and made by unidentified persons, and she argued that no reasonable person in Ahmed's situation would pay any attention to them. I reckoned this heartless, inconsiderate, and nonsensical. I was furious and not thinking nice thoughts. *The masked men never explained their motives to Ahmed. Didn't they know the five protected grounds?*

I was scared now. *Would the BIA run with these arguments?*

*****

On the same day as DHS, Warren submitted to the BIA "Respondent's Brief in Opposition to DHS's Third Appeal." He outlined his arguments in four sections, which I will summarize:

The immigration judge did not err:

A. In her assessment of Ahmed's credibility:

> In hearing after hearing, Ahmed's testimony was responsive, believable, internally consistent, and consistent with the evidence Warren presented in addendum to his legal briefs.

B. In finding the harm sustained by Ahmed rose to the level of persecution:

> Ahmed received two specific, credible, and immediate death threats from Al-Shabaab. Because he applied at

a government hospital, Al-Shabaab took his political opinion as supporting the Somali government. The threat letter was *specific* as they gave it directly to Ahmed. The threat at his sister's house was also specific to Ahmed.

These threats were *credible* because it was from a known terrorist group who attacks and kills people they associate with the Somali government.

The threat letter was *immediate* in that it gave Ahmed only twenty-four to thirty-six hours to leave the country or "face the consequences," which Ahmed understood as meaning they would kill him if he did not comply.

C. In finding Ahmed has a well-founded fear of future persecution, and country conditions in Somalia have not changed:

The judge found Ahmed to have experienced past persecution (the two death threats). Thus, he has a well-founded fear of future persecution because country conditions have not become better but most times have grown worse. And the DHS has itself designated Somalia, one of four countries in the world, to qualify for Temporary Protected Status (TPS) for its citizens.

The Somali police told Ahmed they could not help him, and it was in his best interest just to leave the country.

Opposing support for the Somali government is the primary *motive* to spur Al-Shabaab to acts of terror and murder throughout Somalia. All the country condition reports attest to this.

D. In finding the nexus of the harm suffered by Ahmed was on account of his political opinion, actual or imputed:

Ahmed's name and the names of the other applicants for the government job were posted outside the hospital at the time of his interview. The only thing Ahmed had in common with the other men who were threatened that day at the hospital was that they were all applying for a government position, and as a result, all appeared to support the Somali government.

Within days after receiving DHS's latest "Brief on Appeal," Attorney Jackson submitted "Respondent's Motion to Accept Reply Brief," along with the brief itself, to the BIA. In the motion, Warren expressed his surprise at the many factual inaccuracies and misstatements made by DHS in their brief.

Attorney Jackson pointed out and rebutted eighteen factual inaccuracies or misstatements by DHS. A sample follows:

DHS asserted:

The immigration judge did not make any findings regarding whether the Somali government was unable or unwilling to control Ahmed's persecutors, Al-Shabaab. But Warren argued Ahmed had testified to this, and the judge referred to it and discussed it in her decision. *What more were they looking for?*

Ahmed provided a sworn statement during a credible fear interview before an asylum officer at the border. But Warren pointed out that was not a sworn statement and not a verbatim transcript of the interview, so it was not reliable.

Ahmed testified inconsistently about whether the threat letter was thrown or dropped or handed to Ahmed. But Warren maintained whatever word DHS would like to use to describe the action, it was the same action as giving the letter to him.

Most of the factual inaccuracies and misstatements of DHS were being used as part of the counselor's tactic to find Ahmed's testimony as not trustworthy. And I wondered, *Would any of this sway the BIA? Would Ms. Taylor be called to account for this?*

*****

On Thursday, July 12, 2018, the BIA served a notice of the board's decision to Ahmed, his attorney, and the DHS-ICE Office of Chief Counsel. It named the three panel members of the BIA tribunal, who reviewed the many documents pertaining to Ahmed's case. It contained only four pages and was signed by a member of the tribunal. In it, they repeated the many assertions by DHS in their appeal to the judge's third grant of asylum.

Never once did the board get into the back-and-forth arguments over credibility between DHS and the respondent's attorney. The BIA left Warren's arguments in his brief out of this entirely. The board made its own *de novo review*, not doing its own fact-finding but pointing out and explaining why the immigration judge's findings were clearly erroneous.

The board decided that the immigration judge was in error on multiple counts. First, the BIA disagreed with the judge that the threats Ahmed experienced amounted to persecution because he experienced no physical harm in Somalia, and the threats were vague, lacking in severity, and immediacy.

Second, The BIA disagreed that the masked men gave any motive for the demand that Ahmed leave Somalia because they did not actually say anything when Ahmed received the letter. And further, the masked men offered no explanation to his sister for wanting him to leave Somalia.

Third, the BIA disagreed there was objective evidence to support Ahmed's assumption that because he applied for a job at a government-owned hospital, the men who gave him the letter believed he was a supporter of the Somali government.

Last, the BIA, using their decision on lack of objective evidence, disagreed there was any proof that Ahmed had a well-founded fear of future persecution.

After seeing these arguments in the board's final judgement, I thought that the only way the BIA tribunal would accept the immigration judge's claim of persecution was if Ahmed were flown back to Somalia and killed, and then only if Al-Shabaab claimed responsibility and explained verbally that they did it because Ahmed supported the Somali government. It would help if Al-Shabaab used a more professional letter, in color, so they could better display the crossed-automatic-rifle symbol of Al-Shabaab (Wikipedia 2023).

Sadly, the board's decision ended with an order that the DHS appeal was sustained, the immigration judge's grant of asylum was reversed, and the respondent was to be removed to Somalia.

So there it was—the end of the line. But not quite. Warren could have filed to appeal the BIA's order within thirty days to a higher court, specifically the Federal Circuit Court, but they had a record of siding with the BIA. And if Ahmed took that route and while the appeal was in process, there was no guarantee that he could stay out of jail. Once ICE received a copy of the order for deportation, ICE could again detain him, considering him a flight risk.

We all didn't even discuss appeal to the circuit court as a viable option because going back to jail would break Ahmed's spirit.

Now the doors were closing on alternatives for Ahmed. He had to act quickly.

24

You Will Know What to Do

> When a man is denied the right to live the life he believes in, he has no choice but to become an outlaw.
>
> —Nelson Mandela

Ahmed

I was working now, volunteering at a recycling warehouse. I needed the work because I was going crazy by not being productive. On most days, Dad would drop me off at eight and pick me up at five.

It was a Thursday in the middle of July, pleasantly warm. On my noon lunch break, I went online and checked my status as I usually did every day. But today was different. The worst had happened.

"Hello, Dad, I need you to come pick me up," I said into my phone. "I just checked my status online. They will deport me! I need to come home right away. They'll be coming for me."

"I'll be right there, Ahmed," my dad said. He stopped what he was doing and came right away to get me.

I've been waiting and waiting, and now this. The judgment is clear now: they want to send me back to Somalia. The appeals court tribunal has ruled. They didn't judge the death threats aimed at me as convincing. Over two years, the DHS lawyer had argued three times for my deportation. She tried everything, including lies. Mr. Warren argued well for me to uphold the decision for asylum, to counter whatever Counselor Darcy said. But Helen Alexander, the judge, granted me asylum three times! I was in shock and disbelief. My mind was spinning on what had happened. *It couldn't be real.* I was reaching for courage and control of my feelings as I waited for Dad.

Dad pulled up in his car. He had a worried look. "What can we do now?"

"I have a choice, Dad. Let them take me back to Somalia or escape to Canada and try again for asylum. First, I want to meet with a delegation of Somalis to find out my options. They're from up north, two men and a woman. They're doing some business in town and visiting their Somali friends."

"Where are they now?" asked my dad.

"I don't know, but I can call them, and maybe they'll come pick me up for a meeting."

The Somalis were available. They sent a driver to pick me up, and I was gone for the afternoon. I was introduced to Abdi, but the other two, a husband and wife, greeted me but did not give me their names. The four of us met at a lunch table at the halal grocery downtown. They were kind but serious.

"You should go to Canada," Abdi said, "but that is your choice. We can help you get across the border. We are headed in that direction anyway. If you don't make that choice, ICE will arrest you to deport you—but not right away. First, you'll spend six to nine months in jail."

"Really?" I asked. "I will need time to think about it." Time was moving so fast. I couldn't think clearly and needed to talk with Mom and Dad first.

"Don't think about it too long," the woman said. "Call us in the morning."

A driver brought me home that evening and quickly left.

*****

Mom and Dad and I sat together in the living room. I was feeling dejected; I couldn't smile. "We were sure that the BIA would rule in your favor," Mom said. "This is a shock to your dad and me. We didn't think…were not prepared for this. Whatever you decide, we will help you."

"Thanks, Mom," I said.

"What did they tell you at your meeting?" Dad asked.

"The delegation told me I should go to Canada," I said. "They said my chances were good. They told me they would help me, could take me to the border. There would be others crossing over, seeking asylum, not just me."

"What do you think? It sounds to me like it's your best choice," Dad said.

He spoke calmly, reassuringly. He respected me and always backed me up. I felt like I could tell Mom and Dad anything. They were so caring and kind to me.

"I am tired, so tired of running." I felt tears forming in my eyes. "Let them come pick me up. I miss my wife and my kids. It's been two years since I saw them. They'll want me back. I can take my chances getting out of Somalia and joining them in South Africa once my plane lands."

Mom and Dad waited and considered what I had just said. Finally, Dad said, "You know what will happen. ICE will take you back to jail, and there you will sit for a long time—maybe months, maybe a year—until the plane would have enough Somalis to take you and them back to Somalia. Then you would need to escape from Al-Shabaab. They would know you, even after all this time. Someone will be watching the airport, waiting for those coming back. It wouldn't be safe."

"At least Canada would not be trying to kill you!" Mom said.

"I don't want to go back to jail. I can't go there," I moaned. "But my family."

We had supper and were still talking it over, weighing both sides. After supper, I spoke quietly, "They need an answer by noon tomorrow because they are headed back north. Let me pray on this and sleep on this and decide tomorrow."

"We will pray too," Mom said.
"You will know what to do," Dad said.

*****

Early the following day, I announced, "I have decided to try for asylum in Canada."

Mom got busy packing a small traveling bag with everything she thought I would need. "I have packed little bags for travelers many times," Mom said, "for Mexicans and Central Americans being bussed and deported to their home countries." There was a lot in the bag. Besides the usual toiletries, there were cough drops and tissues, a tiny flashlight, a small water bottle, a washcloth and hand towel, Band-Aids and pain pills, my change of clothing, peanut-filled pretzels, and string cheese—my favorite.

I took Dad aside and told him, "A driver will come very soon to pick me up. They need eight hundred dollars."

"I will be back in half an hour," Dad said.

My dad rushed off to the bank, and while he was gone, the driver of a small white car drove into the driveway and waited. I had never seen him before, but I imagined he was scared and wondering what he had gotten himself into. He was young. But there was no danger yet. I still wore the ankle bracelet.

It was Friday. And the paperwork that said I would be deported would take a few days to get to ICE, and it would soon be the weekend. For once, time was on my side.

Soon, Dad was back and without looking at the driver, gave me one thousand dollars in an envelope. Amid quiet thanks and a tight hug, I quickly shoved the smuggler's fare into my cargo pants pocket.

My mom came to hug me. She was crying. "I'll be okay," I said, "I will call you as soon as I can when I'm safely on the Canada side." Then I stepped into the car and was gone.

I was now on a journey away from my mom and dad, my parents. When I would ever see them again, I didn't know. For almost two years, all that they had worked for so I could one day become an American citizen seemed like a wasted effort. *Could I make it to*

Canada? There was still hope. I left my parents wondering and waiting again.

*****

Abdi had traveled with two others to visit for a few days in Arabella with the Somali community. He was the Somali delegation leader who made final decisions for the group. I was told that our first destination was their home in Minneapolis, a day's journey to the north. And eight of us would cross the border on Saturday night. "For now," Abdi said, "that's all you need to know."

Before we left Arabella, we stopped at Home Depot to buy a garden shear. "We have to get that thing off," Abdi said, pointing to my ankle bracelet. "They won't be able to track you. At first, they'll think the battery is dead. Then they'll want to call you, so we smash the phone as well, and then they can't track you at all."

We rode all day, stopping only for lunch. It was getting late when we arrived at Abdi's house in the big city. We had a little food, rested for a while, and made some plans.

Abdi's friends were gracious. They had good Somali food. A mattress was laid out for me and some others who had gathered. The others appeared excited or gloomy, and I was nervous about the risks I was taking. Apart from introductions and some pleasantries, not much was said.

In the morning, they connected us with a Somali smuggler preparing to take people from Minneapolis to Grand Forks, North Dakota, and from there to the Canadian border. He told me his name, but that wasn't his real name. He used a different name for each trip to the border.

Usually, the smuggler wouldn't take just one person. He would take at least four or more, and we were eight: five men besides me, one woman, and her young son. The smuggler would be the driver. At eight hundred dollars per person, the smuggler was making lots of money just for this trip alone. The other travelers, all Somalis, said hello to each other but did not give each other their full names.

*****

We packed our things and took off for the next leg of the journey. The smuggler had rented a large vehicle, a tinted van with black windows, so people could not see who was inside. And we all agreed that should something happen or should we be stopped, we would say we were going to a wedding. That was our plan. The "wedding" was going to be held in Grand Forks. We reached there around seven in the evening, had something to eat, and began our trip to the border.

We planned our crossing for about midnight. Usually, people cross at night. No one tries a crossing during the day as there is a high presence of ICE personnel on patrol at several spots along the border. They are looking for migrants and drug smugglers, so people have frequently been stopped.

There's a little town just south of the Canadian border, where we stopped briefly on a side street. We could see two look-alike cars in the distance from our car. Our driver identified them. "That's ICE," he said.

He turned the car around and drove out of town into the darkness of the country roads. But we found the ICE cars parked nearby a railroad transit point where he thought we might cross into Canada. So we drove around, around, and around so much that some of the border patrol cars were trying to follow us, which put us at high risk. And we were terrified.

We realized that our luck was running out. And because there was also a young child with us, it would not be easy or safe to cross that night. Since the child's father was not traveling with the mother, there was the possibility of being accused of human trafficking. That would lead to investigations and put us all at risk.

Finally, we all agreed that we had to return to Minneapolis and come back the following night. We really had no choice, the smuggler insisted. He was ready to drop us anywhere at this point. He was frightened too.

25

Days of Uncertainty

Better to die on your feet than to live on your knees.

—Emiliano Zapata

Lucy

Michael listed me with ISAP as one of the people they could call if they needed to get in touch with Ahmed. Whenever Ahmed would not answer his phone, they could phone each of us, in turn, to see where he was and why he was not responding. This never happened until one day in July when I heard they were trying to find him. "Do you know where Ahmed is?" the lady from ISAP asked. "He is not answering his phone."

"No, I haven't seen him in a couple of weeks," I said.

"Thank you," she said and hung up. She sounded sad and betrayed.

I had no idea where he was then, but when I got that call, I started thinking, "Oh, crap, something just went down. Something's going on because Ahmed is usually an extremely responsible person."

I called Michael. "What's going on? What do I need to know? Is Ahmed safe? What's happening? I got a call from the tracker people."

"We all got that call in the last couple of minutes," Michael said. "Elanor did too." Then Michael paused, seeming to catch his breath. "Lucy, you have to come here. We have some very important news."

"What is it?" I asked.

"You and Bill need to come here as soon as you can," was all he would say. Michael, who was usually calm, sounded so desperate.

I gathered up my husband, Bill, and we headed to Annie and Michael's. I drove like a maniac. Annie was sitting in the living room, but Michael was pacing. "Ahmed left today!" Michael said. "They decided to deport him! So he had no choice. He's left with some Somalis to cross into Canada." Michael sat on the couch and lowered his head into his hands.

I was immediately in tears. "They took him away from us!" I cried. "They took him away from us!"

Bill sat there, stunned. None of us talked for some time.

"Yesterday, at noon, Ahmed checked his status online," Michael said. "He found that his case had been decided, and he would be deported. The court gave him thirty days to appeal this decision to a higher Federal court, but he was given no guarantees. If we tried that route, ICE would likely put Ahmed back in jail, but Ahmed told us he couldn't go back there, that it would break his spirit."

"You said Ahmed is headed for Canada," I said. "How does that happen?"

"This afternoon, a car came to our house," Annie said. "Michael hurried off to the bank for some fifties and hundreds to pay the smuggler's fee and some extra funds, and I prepared a small bag with everything he might need for the trip."

"Now we just wait to hear from him," Michael said. "We have no idea what the dangers are, but we know he is not crossing at customs, or they would turn him back. He must cross the border illegally and show up in Canada before they will consider him for asylum. That is how Canadian law works.

"Yet he does not seem fearful. He is traveling with fellow Somalis."

"When will we know his status?" I asked.

"Ahmed said he would call us, and I will let you know as soon as I hear anything from him," Michael said. "We'll stay in touch."

We hugged each other, and Bill and I returned home.

*****

I felt utter shock at this news. It was one of those moments when you want to do it over; you want to stop and say, "Okay, no, no, no, no, this is not real. Let's…let's go back and fix something." But it was with the US government, and they had put it in writing that they would deport him.

I had never felt anger at my government before. I had never felt controlled in this way or my life infringed upon by my government. And there was a moment in all of this when I recognized for the first time in my life that this is what oppression is. This is what oppression feels like. They were taking Ahmed away from Annie and Michael, from my family and me, and it was wrong, and it was unjust, and it was unfair, and there was no reason for it, none whatsoever.

And I didn't know what to do with that anger because there was no one for me to call—maybe the prosecutor, but what would that do? My world shattered that day. I felt resentment, contempt, and disgust that my government was not only doing this to him but doing it to *me*. It was like ripping me apart, pulling me away from my friend, who was like family. There was nothing I could do to change this. I experienced personally the frustration that many feel in this unfair world.

*****

I waited with bated breath as I called Annie and Michael a couple of times every day that weekend. "What have you heard?" I asked. "What have you heard?"

"We haven't heard anything yet," Annie or Michael said. "We're not supposed to hear anything right away. We have to be patient and wait for his call."

And it was so hard to know he was out there and we couldn't help him. And he was trying to get to Canada, but for us, it's so freaking easy. We get in the car, drive across the border, and wave. Yet he had to walk over ankle-breaking ground through cornfields in the dark, looking this way and that, and pray not to be found.

And again, the injustice of why one person has life so easy, and another person not only has it hard but is made to suffer—by what?

By our systems, by our government, by my government. For what? For asylum and a chance in this life? And his best option lies in fleeing from the US government, and he hasn't done the slightest bit wrong? It's just so messed up.

I learned those days the cost of friendship because Ahmed had become my very dear friend. I tied my happiness up with his, attached to his well-being. If he didn't get out and were jailed again, part of me would be jailed too. And if he had to go back and were killed, part of me would die too.

26

He's Not Here Right Now

There are not enough jails, not enough police, not enough courts to enforce a law not supported by the people.

—Hubert H. Humphrey

Michael

I was pacing in my living room. It was Sunday after breakfast, before Annie and I left for church. "Michael, sit," Annie said. "I know you are worried about Ahmed. Let's talk."

"I hope he's okay," I said. "I hope he makes it." I sat and started fidgeting. "But I was wondering, too, about our meeting with ICE. Once they find out from ISAP that Ahmed isn't answering his phone, they're bound to call us and ask us lots of questions. We should talk about this so we're on the same page. What do we tell them?"

"We just say as little as possible—nothing about Canada. Just answer their questions and stick to the facts we know."

"I think you are right. We can just say we haven't seen him since Friday and don't know where he is."

"That's the truth," Annie said. "ICE isn't going to do anything to us. Just relax, Michael."

I kissed her. "I hope Ahmed is okay." Then I laughed. "I have to hand it to Elanor. That night ISAP called everybody, 'I told them nothing!' was all she said. Now she waits like us."

*****

The next day, Monday, July 16, 2018, an ICE agent visited our home. I answered the door. The young man stood back a respectful distance, pulled out his badge and ID, and identified himself as being from ICE, but he wore no uniform and had no weapon. "Is Ahmed here?" he asked.

I sized him up. I saw a well-dressed man, a little like a door-to-door sales agent, with nothing to sell and speaking without emotion. "Ahmed's not here right now," I said.

"When was the last time you saw him?"

"I haven't seen him since last Friday afternoon, when he went off with some friends."

"Thank you." And with that, the officer said no more but turned around and departed.

It amazed me that there was nothing more to discuss. My anxiety was for nothing—all that time spent on Sunday with Annie, exploring and deciding what we would say when ICE came inquiring. It had helped me that Annie had remained calm. It soothed my nerves even while I remained slightly restless. I still did not know the outcome of Ahmed's trip north. *Would Ahmed be arrested by ICE? Would he make it to Canada?*

But the few questions ICE asked showed me we were not responsible for Ahmed's whereabouts. Yes, we had been giving him shelter, food, and other necessities, but ICE had indeed considered Ahmed as "acting on his own recognizance," a circumstance that did not include his sponsors.

However, if ICE had asked for any details that might have put Ahmed in danger, I was prepared to say or do anything necessary to protect him. It was a matter of life or death. Relating simple facts, being truthful, not providing any more information than was asked, and remaining calm were the best plan after all.

27

Home of the Brave

If you want to go quickly, go alone. If you want to go far, go together.

—African Proverb

Ahmed

We drove all night to arrive back in Minneapolis just before sunrise. It was Sunday. We only slept a few hours in the morning. Around three o'clock in the afternoon, the smuggler showed up, and he had made a fateful decision. "Okay, we will not take the mother and child," he said. "As you know, there is a high risk. We will leave them behind, and seven of us will go."

We arrived in the same little town near the border on Sunday night and didn't see those cars moving around this time. "Allāhu Akbar," I said joyfully. "God is most great."

To be safe, the smuggler took the long road across the river, which was very low and empty at some points, and he just dropped us in an open field. We all got out, dug out our bags, and started walking north.

"From where you are dropped, walk five miles north," the smuggler told us earlier that day. "You will know what is north if you see the North Star. If it's cloudy, look for a tree in the distance that makes a right angle to the road you are on. Once you have walked for two hours, call 9-1-1, and they'll come and pick you up. Don't be afraid. This is not the first time we've done this, you know." But it was cloudy, and where we were let out, the road had just ended.

We headed for what we thought was north and walked over the mostly bumpy ground. We were blessed that no moon was shining even above the thin clouds that blocked our sight of the stars. It was midnight again and very dark. I pulled out the tiny flashlight Mom packed for me. There wasn't one on the cheap phone I carried. We walked what we supposed was five miles over fields and through trees. The ground was relatively level, but the uneven terrain and the darkness slowed us. After about two hours, we stopped.

The smuggler had given me a "burner phone," a cheap prepaid one, because I found out very early that I was the only one who spoke English. I became the interpreter for the group. I called 9-1-1 and waited for the answer. "Hello," is all I said.

But the man who answered didn't sound Canadian. Somehow, it seemed he knew we'd be calling. "Where are you guys?" he asked.

I quickly hung up. "I don't think we're far enough," I said in Somali to the group. "We need to walk more, far enough to be sure that we're in Canada."

We trudged on, twice as much distance and time as we had already come. It was important for us to be sure. We were walking on the darker side of a road but very far from the road where no one could see us. We walked in farm fields and sometimes in trees.

I watched the strength of the signal on the phone. I saw it slowly drop in strength and then start rising again. Once I believed we were finally in Canada, I let our group know and called 9-1-1 once again.

"What's wrong?" a woman asked, in a heavy accent that I took for Canadian.

"We seek asylum in Canada," I said.

"How many?"

"There are six of us from Somalia. Am I talking to—"

"Are there any children or women with you?"

"No," I said.

"Where are you?" She sounded calm but alert.

"I think we are about five miles north of the border and a couple miles west of the river if we walked in a straight line. We are on the east side of a plowed field near some trees."

"Walk out into the field so we can spot you. Wait there. We will come. We'll be there very soon," she said. "Do you have a flashlight?"

"Yes," I said, then I thanked her and hung up. I knew they could call us now that they had our cell number. We waited about a half hour and saw two pairs of headlights bouncing over the field toward where we were waiting, our little flashlight flashing.

Two SUVs stopped near us, and four officers, very big men, got out. They had large flashlights and approached us. I noticed they had CBP (Canadian Border Patrol) patches on their shoulders. And because of our experience in the US, we all raised our hands and were ready to be handcuffed.

"No, don't do that," one of them said. "This is Canada. We're not going to handcuff you. You are coming with us."

And I could see how happy everyone was. We were all exhausted, but relief showed on each of our faces. We had eluded ICE and gotten safely into Canada! The US would no longer be chasing us.

I relaxed then, took a deep breath, and let it all out. A smile slowly rose on my face, and tears started to form. I was free!

*****

They took the six of us to Emerson, Manitoba, the nearest Canadian port of entry. The US Border Patrol offices were right next door. Because it was late and everyone was tired, they gave us blankets and food. They knew people had different religions and were limited in what they could eat, so they gave us vegetarian food, mainly noodles. They were caring and friendly in their treatment of us.

Outside the border patrol facility was a modified shipping container with windows and a door cut into one side. They housed us there. So we ate some food, lay on cots, and quickly slept.

In the morning, they conducted interviews. Everyone was called in one by one. Pictures were taken. Fingerprints were taken. We filled out many forms. They verified the information we gave them with the US database to ensure everything matched.

When it was my turn, the lady said that she had contacted the US authorities. "US Immigration told me that you have legal status in the US," she said. "Either you go back there *now*, or we keep you up to seven days and then send you back to the US but with no legal representative."

"That's not right," I said. "I have *no* legal status. I have been ordered removed to Somalia. And the US Immigration was not telling the truth."

She sat there quietly for a few seconds. "Okay…wait. I'm going to double-check." Then she got up and left the room.

It was minutes but seemed like hours as I waited. I was apprehensive. *Maybe it was a setup.* If I were sent back to the US, I would be detained, and then… My stomach was churning.

The lady came back and sat at her desk. "I am sorry," she said. "No, you were mistaken for someone else. Indeed, you were ordered for removal from the US. Welcome to Canada! Officially."

*****

By midafternoon, around three o'clock, they gave everyone his file, which included a picture ID card with the status "Eligible for Asylum."

Soon, an Arab man, a taxi driver who worked with immigration, came to pick us up. We were all brought to the Salvation Army in Winnipeg and assigned to beds. And there, I met other immigrants and shared a room with two men from Eritrea.

I borrowed a phone and called my parents. I was standing by my bed. I couldn't sit. I was very excited. I couldn't wait to tell them the good news. Then I called Zoya. We shared our deep joy that I was safe in Canada. It was quiet for a moment, and then I heard her crying. It was after midnight in South African time, so we didn't talk long. After my call, she woke up our kids and gave them the good news. Last, I called my sister Fawzia. I wanted her to know right away.

Later that evening, I went to buy pizza with one of my roommates at midnight. We couldn't sleep. And besides, we were celebrating! It was exhilarating for me that here I was on Canadian soil as a free man, and within one day, I could walk around and buy what I wanted. It felt so natural, so normal. Nobody was checking on me. I felt total freedom.

*****

The following morning, I walked to the immigration offices for a seven-thirty appointment. The man who did my interview was compassionate and understanding as he had all my information. At the end of the interview, he gave me a four-year residence status document and referred me to another office where I would have a caseworker. Once I met her, I was all set up. She opened a bank account for me, applied for my work permit, and made some essential job references—all within three days! *Have I been in Canada for three years or three days?* Those were the most amazing days for me in Canada.

28

Front Door or Back Door

> The fact is, Canadians understand that immigration, that people fleeing for their lives, that people wanting to build a better life for themselves and their kids is what created Canada, it's what created North America.
>
> —Justin Trudeau (2016)

Michael

Monday, the same day the man from ICE visited, but later that afternoon, at about 4:00 p.m., I got a call from Ahmed that I will never forget. "I'm calling from Canada," Ahmed said. "I finally made it! I can't talk long. I'm using someone else's phone. I wanted to let you and Mom know first."

"Thank God! Oh, that's so wonderful!" I said. "Is everything okay?"

"We crossed the border, called 9-1-1, and the officers welcomed us. For only that night, I was in detention. They asked me about my story, and they all felt so sorry for me. I'm now in Winnipeg, and they are setting me up in an apartment. They will assign me a case manager very soon."

I could not believe the good news. I was feeling so thrilled, and I wanted to share this with Annie. "Your mom is not here right now.

She will be back this evening," I said. "She will be overjoyed at your news. Does Zoya know? You said we were the first ones you called."

"I will call her now, and I will talk to you again soon."

At seven thirty that evening, Ahmed called again. This time, Annie was home and answered his call. Annie talked for a long while, laughed, and cried.

I listened in. After a bit, I went into another room and called my friend Lucy to give her the excellent news. She sounded so relieved and thankful that Ahmed was safe. Then I called Elanor, Martin, Charlie, and Marie—all the friends and sponsors on Ahmed's journey. Everyone celebrated.

It is so hard to describe the feeling. Ahmed was at last on a clear path to asylum! Over two years of fighting for this in the US, only to be rejected, and then to be welcomed with open arms in Canada.

*****

At the immigration offices in Winnipeg, where people were going and coming every day, Ahmed got the news that the Canadian authorities had refused asylum to the mom and her son, who had not been with them on the Sunday night border crossing. Within the same week, a different smuggler took them to the border and dropped them right at the Canadian port of entry. Then he made a U-turn to return to the US. He could do this legally.

But anyone who tried to claim asylum at the border checkpoint would not be accepted. You had to come in the back door (cross into Canada illegally) as an "irregular migrant," as Ahmed had done, then you could be accepted for asylum. That's the Canadian immigration law that Canadians wanted to change but hadn't done so far. Some agreements had to be honored between the US and Canada. Ahmed and the other Somalis were told this, but she wouldn't believe it. She must have been desperate. Her smuggler should have known this too. Maybe he did, but he had already pocketed the smuggler's fee.

So a CBP officer took them next door to US Immigration and handed them over to ICE, and ICE arrested her with her son and took them away. If Ahmed's case had been still undecided (with the possibility of asylum in the US), instead of Ahmed being under orders to be deported, the same thing would have happened to him. That's the cruel part of the immigration agreements between the two countries.

*****

In the coming weeks, they assigned an immigration lawyer to Ahmed and together prepared for his first asylum hearing. It would take more waiting, but he felt assured (we all did) of the favorable outcome this time.

I had and will always have the greatest respect for Ahmed. He was willing to do whatever it took, whatever was in his power, to secure safety, freedom, and a better life for his family. He followed through and never wavered. The eventual outcome was not what any of us expected, but I felt that he achieved what he set out to do.

Together with Annie and a compassionate community, I had done my part to help Ahmed's dream come true. As I contemplated the role I played, I thought of the famous *The Star Thrower* story:

> He stooped again, oblivious of my curiosity, and skipped another star neatly across the water. "The stars," he said, "throw well. One can help them." He looked full at me with a faint question kindling in his eyes, which seemed to take on the far depths of the sea. (Eiseley 1978, 172)

29

Export and Import

> If you come at four in the afternoon,
> I'll begin to be happy by three.
>
> —Antoine de Saint-Exupéry, *The Little Prince*

Annie

November 10, 2018

    Almost four months went by since we had last seen Ahmed. We made a plan to visit him in Winnipeg, Manitoba, over a weekend in November. Michael and I would drive our Camry, and Lucy and Lily, their small SUV. We needed two cars for two reasons. First, Michael and I were planning to donate our fifteen-year-old car to Ahmed and then ride back in Lucy's car. Second, the load of luggage, half of which was stuff for Ahmed, would not fit into one car with four passengers.

    Ahmed had left behind clothing and belongings he had acquired during his five months with us. Friends had donated lots of stuff for him too. So we packed up two large suitcases of Ahmed's possessions and loads of boxes of donated items. I separated things into two categories and made a spreadsheet of their values. It was to ensure that we could pay the import taxes at Canadian customs without hassle.

Michael had spent many hours researching exporting and importing, the import tax, and the papers needed for the US and Canada. The forms were fewer and more straightforward because the car was over fifteen years old. He had also printed out Google Maps images of the border crossing, showing the rooftops of the customs buildings, parking lots, and roadways. He knew we needed to stop at the rear door of US Customs first and was worried we might pass it by. That's the way Michael was. He was prepared for everything.

The day we picked for our journey was unfortunate. That Saturday morning, it began to snow early. By the time Michael and I departed, four inches had covered the roadways. It was tough for our Camry with front-wheel drive and with the load balanced toward the rear. The many SUVs with their four-wheel drive seemed to laugh in the snow. It took two hours to get on the freeway. Michael was driving and turning into a nervous wreck as he approached the bottom of steep hills at red lights with many cars on the one-lane road stopping and starting. Would he make the next leg? He stopped with plenty of room to get started at a green light. The intersections were glazing over. When he finally made the freeway, he said his neck was stiff as a board.

Lucy had no real problem. She and Lily couldn't leave until noon. But they lived near the freeway, and by then, much of the roadways were plowed. They had four-wheel drive too. They would meet us in Grand Forks, and we would stay in a hotel on our first night.

We got an early start the next day, a Sunday, to avoid the usual border traffic. We were headed to Winnipeg, a city of immigrants, where Ahmed was living and acclimating. Everything was in order when we reached the border and checked with US Customs. They cleared us to proceed.

Michael was driving, and we were in the lead car. We stopped at the Canadian drive-up window. "Have you anything to declare?" the customs officer said.

"Yes," Michael said. "We have brought a bunch of things for a friend and are also gifting this car to him."

"Who is it for?"

"It's for a man named Ahmed, a recent traveler to Canada, a refugee seeking asylum."

"Pull up over there. Someone will help you," the officer said.

We parked our cars, opened our trunks, and unloaded the suitcases and boxes. A couple of officers came out and took all the stuff into the building. It was too cold to do their inspections outside. They were looking for documents, any documents that pertained to Ahmed.

Michael and I took our paperwork inside while the others milled about the parking lot. The customs building was not crowded. Maybe two other parties were being served at what looked like bank teller windows. The customs officials were friendly. No one was rushed. It was a Sunday. Michael laid his papers out and asked about some blank lines he still had to fill in. He learned he would be both an exporter and importer and was given one more document to complete.

While he was busy with that, I stood at another window and showed them my spreadsheet. The customs officer was impressed. "Take this over to the cashier," he said.

I joined Michael at the payment table, and Michael paid the VAT for the car. It wasn't too bad. As we turned to leave, I said, "What about the donated items we are importing?"

"Don't worry about that. It's okay." The official smiled.

That surprised me. I could only guess why we were not asked to pay more. Perhaps they appreciated our honesty, not hiding anything. Perhaps we had already paid enough.

Outside, I found Lucy checking in with her husband. Before she finished her call, she said, "I love you."

The chief officer was walking by and grinned and said, "I didn't know you cared that much for me." He hadn't seen her cell phone. He gave a little laugh when Lisa showed it to him.

"Here, you want some M&M's?" She held a big bag in her hand. She was sharing the candy with everyone who walked by.

I thought about how easy all this was. It was easier to move an old car across the border than a person, a person needing sanctuary. Just fill out paperwork and pay taxes, no waiting patiently for months or years.

As we all packed up, the chief came back out with a stack of letters that Ahmed had saved and I had packed for him. Over sixty letters from me, still in envelopes, bound carefully in twine and kept safe—from all those days Ahmed was in jail—they were precious to him.

"What about those?" I asked the chief.

"Oh, these? These are just love letters," and he handed them to me.

*****

We found a parking spot downtown at about noon and paid for parking with a credit card at a street-side kiosk. We walked a few blocks and found Ahmed outside his apartment building. He was facing the other way, looking for us. We snuck up behind him and tapped him on the shoulder. When he turned around, we all started saying hello and laughing. Then the one-by-one hugging commenced.

Ahmed was renting a room in a high-rise apartment building. We carried the stuff we brought up in the elevator, and Ahmed unpacked a few things. He was glad to get the letters back, his laptop, but especially the prayer mat that my sister had made for him. We all did not stay there long. We didn't want to be a bother for the lady whose apartment it was.

After parking our gifted car in the high-rise garage, we managed to find our Airbnb a few miles away. It was a house in a quiet neighborhood.

It was so good to see Ahmed. We caught up with all the news: how Ahmed was faring, what Canada immigration had told him, and how his family was doing in South Africa. Michael was especially interested in Ahmed's escape across the border. When Ahmed told that story, we all showed amazement at how dangerous it had been—how close Ahmed was to being stopped by the US border patrol, handed over to ICE, and put back in jail. His trip could easily have ended in disaster.

Ahmed then took us out to see the sights around Winnipeg. There was a park with some restaurants and Canada's version of a shopping mall. We walked outside, strolled around, and enjoyed each other's company. There was a light dusting of snow. We saw parents with kids with ice skates slung over their shoulders, heading somewhere to enjoy the mild—for Winnipeg—midfall weather. Lucy bought some warm pants for Ahmed while we looked in the shops. We had a meal at a semi-outdoor café. It was pleasant, and the food was good and plenty.

That evening, we were back at Ahmed's apartment. The lady was not there, so we had the place to ourselves. Lily had gone off somewhere to scout out the town. She was a high school junior and entirely independent. Meanwhile, the four of us had an intimate conversation. We packed in all the things we had wanted to say to him. We sought to share in his happiness. We wanted to see the smile on his face. He had fulfilled his dream. He was safe now, and we knew his family would someday join him.

It overjoyed Ahmed to see us. And he kept expressing his thanks for all we had done for him.

The next day, our day of departure, we found a Tim Hortons café, had a good cup of coffee, and joined Ahmed in ordering cinnamon rolls, a step up for him from the honey buns he bought in jail. We said our goodbyes and headed back south.

"What did you think of Winnipeg, Lily?" Michael asked.

"Kind of like a bigger Arabella, but colder."

"What about Ahmed?"

"He seemed very happy, very grateful, probably still adjusting, especially to the cold."

When we filled up with gas in Winnipeg, it surprised us there was no self-service. A man with a heavy accent, who sounded like he had newly arrived from Scotland, pumped the gas. And Michael quietly asked his fellow travelers, "Should I tip him?"

Lily was adamant. "No, he won't want American dollars!"

But Michael gave him two dollars, which the serviceman gladly accepted with a big smile.

This time, we drove nonstop to Arabella. Lily took over driving quite a bit. She was practicing with her permit. Her driving kept Michael awake—no close calls, but her mother made light of a few episodes of swerving.

*****

Ahmed is flourishing, his hope for freedom a cherished reality. In all ways possible, he is making Canada his home. Different rules, cultures, and geography are nothing compared to the harsh realities he left behind. He is out of the grasp of terrorists, smugglers, cartels, jailers, immigration courts, and the crushing weight of uncertainty. I celebrate his freedom with relief and joy.

And now I am deeply grateful, grateful for Ahmed. His happiness has uplifted my spirit. He crossed the finish line, and I will never be the same.

30

Relationship

My brother has the coolest sister. I'm just saying.

—Leslie Nevala

Lucy

It was not until November that we could finally drive up to see him. Every week, we would say, "Well, when can we go? When's the plan?" And it was a joyful trip because we knew he was safe, and Canada was working out for him. Lily had her first long highway journey as a new driver with a permit.

Michael was his usual self. He had specked out the border crossing on Google Maps. I kidded him about that, but we all appreciated how smoothly it went. And here we were in Canada. The land was very flat, mostly grainfields that were all harvested by now. Here and there were thin lines of trees, windbreaks to keep the soil in place.

When we got to Winnipeg, we drove downtown. The Canadian government had arranged a place for Ahmed to stay. He was so proud of it. He had a bedroom and shared a kitchen and sitting room in an apartment in a high-rise building with delightful views.

Ahmed was free. He could come and go as he pleased and eagerly awaited a job placement. And he was so happy again, just so, so happy. It was wonderful to see him and have a meal with him.

And it felt like a family reunion. It really did. And I am amazed at the difference a government response can make. The US paid thousands of dollars to keep a man who wasn't a criminal in jail for twenty-plus months, but the Canadian government immediately got him an apartment and helped him find work to be productive in their society, and it just made so much more sense. Our system, how it played out for him, was just crazy.

After the trip to see Ahmed, we started thinking more and more about his family. We began waiting for the day when his wife and kids could join him. We knew it would be a slow process, but Ahmed's positive energy never left him.

*****

Ahmed and I now feel like we are brother and sister. We are close in age, and he addresses Annie as *Mom* and Michael as *Dad*. Being part of one extensive family is what it feels like. We text and call each other, and every time we do, there is somehow a spiritual connection. He knows his new extended family loves him, and we know he immensely loves us. Despite the years, the miles, the cultural barriers, the uncertainty, and whatever you want to call the difficulties, I have been blessed and continue to be blessed to have someone of his caliber in my life.

And I can't wait for Ahmed's family to be together again. That's my greatest hope right now: for him to realize the joy that comes from overcoming everything to provide a life for his family, for which he has struggled for so long.

*****

Some people believe immigrants are different in some undefined way, and they are uncomfortable with that difference. Despite that, others think we should welcome them, that we are a country of immigrants, and at least we ought to tolerate them. How many people truly realize that *the immigrant* has the same capacity to love and share all their unique gifts? How many consider that *the immigrant* might change our lives and make us better people?

Yet that's what Ahmed did. I became a better person because of him. He made me better because he made me recognize the blindness that I had toward my justice system. I came to realize the power of faith and joy and persistence through his example. He inspired me in so many ways with his love for his family, the lengths he would go to keep himself and his family safe. Still, more than anything, he filled in corners of my life with his faith and kept me going when I needed it, reminding me I can get through anything because he can get through anything.

I hope more people will realize the giftedness of the immigrant and the joy they can bring to our world, our lives, and our families.

Epilogue

> Life is like riding a bicycle. To keep your
> balance, you must keep moving.
>
> —Albert Einstein

Ahmed

On July 19, 2019, the Canadian court granted me asylum! Three weeks before that, Mr. Warren, my US immigration lawyer, wrote up a very thorough letter, which I think was beneficial to my case for asylum in Canada (see "Appendix C: Regarding Ahmed").

One year later, although we had been in touch by phone every week, Mom sent me a letter to commemorate the fateful decision that put me on this fresh path.

> July 15, 2020
> Hello, Ahmed,
>
> Just a note to say hello!
> Today is the eve of July 16, the day [two years ago] you left the U.S.A. and headed to Canada. Such a courageous, big-time turning point in your life. It would be interesting to write down for posterity not just what happened, but also the strong and varied feelings on that remarkable journey. It will be a landmark story for your grandchildren and great-grandchildren.

Know you are loved and missed by many here in Arabella.

Mom

And another year after that, on July 8, 2021, Canada granted my family and me permanent residency! It had taken three years and put me one step closer to full citizenship in Canada. But my family was still waiting—"in process"—on the threshold. So many were passing through the doorway ahead of them. They had been waiting longer. The door seemed closed for them and locked for now, and as we often heard in East Africa, "Can't get in? The man with the key is gone."

In September of that same year, I decided it was best for my family to move to Uganda. Johannesburg was becoming more and more dangerous with increasing crime and xenophobia. Besides that, I feared corruption might extend to the Canadian Embassy, and they may be holding back my family. *Were they expecting a bribe?*

My parents had a friend and former colleague in Kampala, Uganda. Annie gave me his name and phone number. Joseph was happy to help. Zoya contacted him when they arrived, and together, they found an apartment and bought what they needed to set up the household. Joseph knew the area, had contacts, and found them a safe place to live.

*****

In December 2022, my employer gave me two weeks' vacation. I received two more while they shut work down for the holidays. A full month! I planned a trip to see my family. Zoya knew, but we kept it a surprise for our kids. They were told only that a family relative was visiting for a day. Zoya needed an excuse to do extra shopping and prepare without the kids becoming suspicious.

As I dragged my two bags through the airport in Entebbe, my kids were looking to see who this man could be. Talia, my oldest, was the first person who recognized me. And although a large group of people were waiting outside, Talia just screamed. And all three kids ran to me, giving me one of the longest hugs I could ever remember. They wouldn't even let Zoya hug me. They hugged me for five minutes, touching my body and saying, "Is it really you, Dad? Is it you, or is it just our eyes?"

I couldn't talk. I was numb, and then Zoya came to greet me. It was beautiful, and I felt filled up to overflowing, something I will never forget for the rest of my life.

Yes, I took so much stuff for them: chocolates, clothes, shoes, cell phones, watches—everything I could afford. And they were all happy. It was a celebration! The clothes I brought fit them well. So did the shoes. The cell phones were much needed and appreciated.

My kids wanted to know everything! "Tell us, Dad," they said. "Tell us about your journey from South Africa to Somalia, to Canada, and what happened in between, especially the US jail. And what happened that they had kept you for nineteen months? What was your life like? What did you do? How did you spend your days? How did you keep your head above the water? What were you thinking every day? How was the US? How did you meet your dad and mom?" And I believe it almost took two nights because I couldn't answer all the questions in one night, and I was tired.

I also asked them how their life was without me in South Africa. And we spent the whole time together and just enjoyed each other's company. We made many memories, like eating with Chinese chopsticks, making some little animals from modeling clay, and taking pictures to see who made the best animal. I challenged my son to see how many push-ups each of us could do. He was as big as me now. And my youngest daughter had grown so much in six years. Now she was a young lady of seventeen.

But one thing was bugging them. When I left South Africa, the kids were asleep and later were unhappy that I went while they were sleeping, and so now they asked, "Why did you leave without hugging us and kissing us? Why did you go without saying goodbye?"

I apologized, and I explained, "Back then, you were young. You couldn't comprehend, and I couldn't take an image with me of all of you crying. I wouldn't have been able to turn my back on you and walk away, so I left in darkness, and only your mother went with me to the gate to board my flight."

But now they were grown up, and so they understood and appreciated what I did.

When it was finally time for me to leave to go back to Canada, Zoya again rented a van and hired a driver for the journey from Kampala to Entebbe. This time, Talia stayed behind. Zoya sat in the back with me. We were holding hands. Everyone was quiet.

We found a parking spot and walked to the door of the terminal. We said goodbye to each other with lots of hugs and kisses and tears. I picked up my bags, now much lighter, and turned away. They watched me go but only left when I disappeared into the airport.

*****

I have a country now. Canada has been good to me. I feel safe, no longer looking over my shoulders. For all this and more, my heart is full of gratitude.

I have a good job, am being productive and rewarded for my efforts. But I live simply. My wages are more than enough for me. I send all I can spare to Africa for my wife and kids.

But I am alone. I am a husband and father but over a great distance. My December visit was wonderful but reminded me of all that was missing from my life.

Zoya and the kids are safe but still waiting, their lives on hold. Even though they received permanent residency at the same time as me, they are waiting for clearance to come to Canada. There are a few procedures to follow once they arrive.

For now, eight thousand miles lie between them and me. Our expectation for one day being together has stretched thin, like the chain of communication that links our twice-daily conversations. Their official status with Canada is "in process" as they move in a queue shared by over a million others.

"Allāhu Akbar," I say joyfully. "God is most great." Hope has been given to me. That day will come—I am certain—that we will be together again.

Postscript

Ahmed, as the Canadian sponsor for his family, tried everything to speed the process for his family's relocation to Canada. He regularly contacted the local MP (Member of Parliament), hired an immigration attorney from Toronto, and monthly contacted the Canadian Embassy in East Africa.

Then, on November 17, 2023, an official letter came to Zoya, attached to an email. The letter was from the High Commission of Canada in Dar es Salaam, Tanzania. Ahmed's family could now move to Canada!

The letter stated in part: "We are currently processing your application for permanent residency. You now qualify to receive pre-arrival services to help you prepare for your new life in Canada."

They would wait just a little longer. But they would be busy attending orientation, collecting documentation on their educational and employment histories, receiving medical checkups, and getting Canadian visas.

Then the big day. Ahmed's family would travel with escorts in a group of about thirty refugees and be received at long last by Ahmed in a Canadian Province and city of their choosing.

Finally, back together again after almost eight years, their new life would begin.

*****

TIMOTHY LEACOCK

The Land of the Sugar Maple Tree

Come away, come away to Canada
Where the sugar maple grows so free;
Inhale the wholesome air of freedom
And sip nectar from the sugar maple tree.

Our fertile land of river, lake and prairie
Is the ideal place for you and me;
Where the birds are always sweetly singing
And our British law is Liberty.

We have spruce and pine in good and plenty;
Elm, ash and birch grow vigorously;
But the nearest one to our loving hearts
Is the beautiful sugar maple tree.

The singing birds of brightest plumes
Find homes in all their branches.
You too can have a bower built
Where each one has such chances.

Oh we are a mighty nation
And prolific with wheat kings.
We are filled with jubilation
That wealth and comfort brings.

Canada published this poem in a promotional pamphlet created by the Department of Agriculture in 1906.

Appendix A

Al-Shabaab

This extraction from a report about Al-Shabaab—who they are, their history, and operations—is from the National Counter-Terrorism Center (NCTC) website:

The Harakat Shabaab al-Mujahidin—commonly known as al-Shabaab—was the militant wing of the Somali Council of Islamic Courts that took over most of southern Somalia in the second half of 2006. Despite the group's defeat by Somali and Ethiopian forces in 2007, al-Shabaab—a clan-based insurgent and terrorist group—has continued its violent insurgency in southern and central Somalia. The group has exerted temporary and, at times, sustained control over strategic locations in those areas by recruiting, sometimes forcibly, regional sub-clans and their militias, using guerrilla warfare and terrorist tactics against the Federal Government of Somalia (FGS), African Union Mission in Somalia (AMISOM) peacekeepers, and nongovernmental aid organizations.

As evidenced by the constant levels of infighting among leadership, al-Shabaab is not centralized or monolithic in its agenda or goals.

Its rank-and-file members come from disparate clans, and the group is susceptible to clan politics, internal divisions, and shifting alliances. Most of its fighters are predominantly interested in the nationalistic battle against the FGS and not supportive of global jihad. Al-Shabaab's senior leaders remain affiliated with al-Qa'ida.

Al-Shabaab has claimed responsibility for many bombings—including various types of suicide attacks—in Mogadishu and in central and northern Somalia, typically targeting Somali government officials, AMISOM, and perceived allies of the FGS. (NCTC 2023)

From this report, one can see that Al-Shabaab is made up of many conflicting groups. Thus, its agenda, motives, and operations are unpredictable. Nevertheless, and over the course of many years, this insurgent group has proved deadly.

Appendix B

Types of Asylum

The following explanation of the various types of asylum, and other forms of protection, is from the UNHCR-USA website:

> To apply for asylum in the U.S., you must be physically present in the U.S. or be seeking entry into the U.S. at a port of entry.
>
> Forms of asylum
>
> There are two paths to claim asylum in the U.S. The affirmative asylum process is for individuals who are not in removal proceedings and the defensive asylum process is for individuals who are in removal proceedings. Removal proceedings are when the United States government orders that you be removed (deported) from the United States:
>
> - Affirmative Asylum: A person who is not in removal proceedings may proactively apply for asylum through U.S. government, with the U.S. Citizenship and Immigration Services (USCIS), a division of the Department of

Homeland Security (DHS). If the USCIS asylum officer does not grant the asylum application, the applicant is referred to removal proceedings, where he or she may renew the request for asylum through the defensive process and appear before an immigration judge.

- Defensive Asylum: A person who is in removal proceedings may apply for asylum defensively by filing the application with an immigration judge at the Executive Office for Immigration Review (EOIR) in the Department of Justice. In other words, asylum is applied for "as a defense against removal from the U.S."

Individuals are in removal proceedings after being apprehended (taken into custody) in the United States or at a U.S. port of entry without proper legal documents or in violation of their immigration status. This also applies to those who were apprehended by U.S. Customs and Border Protection (CBP) trying to enter the United States without proper documentation, were placed in the expedited removal process, and were found to have a credible fear of persecution or torture by an Asylum Officer.

In both the affirmative and defensive process, individuals have a right to a lawyer. However, unlike the criminal court system in the U.S., the U.S. government does not provide lawyers for individuals in immigration court, even if they are unable to hire a lawyer on their own.

Other forms of protection: Withholding of Removal and CAT

There are other forms of protection in the United States besides defensive asylum. Withholding of Removal and the Convention Against Torture (CAT) are other defenses against removal. The same form (form I-589) is used to apply for Withholding of Removal, CAT, and defensive asylum.

Withholding of removal

Even if you do not qualify for asylum, you may still be eligible for withholding of removal. If you are granted withholding of removal, you will not qualify for a green card but you will be allowed to re-main and work lawfully in the United States. To win Withholding of Removal, you must demonstrate that it is more likely than not that you will suffer future persecution if returned to your home country because of your race, religion, nationality, membership in a particular social group, or political opinion. The standard of proof for withholding of removal is higher than for asylum: you need to show that there is more than a 50 percent chance you will be persecuted.

Relief under the Convention Against Torture (CAT)

If you fear torture in your home country, you may qualify for another form of relief under the CAT. You must prove that you are more likely than not to be tortured either directly by the government or with the "acquiescence" of the government if returned to your country of origin. "Acquiescence" generally means the government is aware of the torture but does not try to stop it. (UNHCR 2018)

Since Ahmed did not have "proper legal documents"—that is, he did not have a US visa or other documents allowing him to stay in the US, even temporarily—he could not qualify for "Affirmative Asylum" and was subject to detention.

For Ahmed to qualify for "Withholding of Removal," he needed to show a higher standard of proof (greater than fifty percent) of *future* persecution, but there was no requirement of proving to have suffered *past* persecution. And this status would be much less desirable because the US government could revoke withholding of removal should his home country conditions improve.

Appendix C

Regarding Ahmed

The following is from a letter sent to Ahmed to be given to his Canadian attorney:

July 1, 2019
RE: Ahmed Mahamed Absame
To Whom It May Concern,

I represented Mr. Absame for nearly two years in his immigration proceedings in the U.S. before the Immigration Court and Board of Immigration Appeals ("BIA").

Mr. Absame was granted asylum on three separate occasions by the Immigration Judge, but the U.S. Department of Homeland Security ("DHS") appealed each time and was finally successful in overturning his grant of asylum at the BIA on July 12, 2018.

While we certainly disagree with the BIA's ruling on its merits, we have further reason to believe that this decision and especially the unprecedented DHS efforts to appeal the Immigration Judge's grant of asylum were politically motivated by our own government.

I have been an immigration attorney for over ten years and have never seen the DHS appeal an Immigration Judge's grant of immigration relief more than once, and that has only been on three prior occasions.

When Mr. Absame was granted asylum for a third time in December 2017, I called our deputy chief counsel for the DHS, who is responsible for all removal/deportation cases in our local Immigration Court, to ask if they would be appealing a third time and why they were choosing to litigate this case more than any other I have ever experienced. He responded that "we are fighting all Somali cases now to the very end, and I assure you we will win." This chilling statement just so happened to coincide with President Trump's efforts to implement multiple travel bans or, more accurately, "Muslim" bans which, except theoretically if an extremely limited waiver is granted that neither I nor my colleagues have ever witnessed being approved, prevent the admission of all immigrants from certain countries including Somalia. Sure enough, of course, the DHS did keep appealing and were finally successful at the BIA.

There is no doubt in my mind that if Mr. Absame were not Somali, the DHS would not have appealed his case, and the BIA would not have sustained their appeal. Mr. Absame meets the definition of a refugee under U.S. and international law.

My hope is that your country will do what mine did not and finally award him the permanent asylum status he deserves. He would be a great asset to Canada with his intelligence and yearning for higher education.

Please let me know if you require further information or documentation. Thank you for your time and attention to this important matter.

Mr. Warren Jackson
Attorney at Law

Reference List

Eiseley, Loren. *The Star Thrower*. New York: Harcourt Brace & Company. 1978.
ICE. "Detention Management." Accessed 2022. https://www.ice.gov/detain/detention-management.
Immigration, Refugees and Citizenship Canada. Accessed 2018. https://www.canada.ca/en/immigration-refugees-citizenship/services/refugees.html.
NCTC. "Al-Shabaab." Accessed 2023. https://www.dni.gov/nctc/groups/al_shabaab.html.
UNHCR USA. "Types of Asylum." 2018. https://help.unhcr.org/usa/applying-for-asylum/types-of-asylum.
Wikipedia. "Al-Shabaab (Militant Group)." 2023. https://en.wikipedia.org/wiki/Al-Shabaab_%28militant_group%29.

Printed in the USA
CPSIA information can be obtained
at www.ICGtesting.com
JSHW080438230124
55619JS00001B/7

9 798891 121669